Binary Tree Problems

Must for Interviews and Competitive Coding

- **Aditya Chatterjee, Srishti Guleria, Ue Kiao**

About this book

This book "**Binary Tree Problems**" is carefully crafted to present you the knowledge and practice (around the data structure, *Binary Tree*) needed to ace Coding Interviews and Competitive Coding Contests.

The book takes you through the fundamentals of Binary Tree, presents how to implement it in a good and secure way, make you practice key problems, present variants like Threaded Binary Tree, Binary Space Partitioning Tree, Skewed Binary Tree, AVL Tree, Treap and much more.

The content covered is deep and is not covered by any other standard book.

Each chapter is followed by a brief note of insight which wraps up your though in the correct direction and is a feast for budding **Independent Researchers**.

If you aspire you to a good Software Developer, you should definitely get this book. You will be prepared to apply Binary Tree is designing solutions to key real life problems like designing an Excel sheet or making Game Graphics render fast.

If you face any doubt, you can reach us by email: team@opengenus.org

Authors: **Aditya Chatterjee; Srishti Guleria; Ue Kiao;**

About the Authors:

Aditya Chatterjee is an Independent Researcher and the Founding Member of OPENGENUS, a scientific community focused on Computing Technology.

Srishti Guleria is a Maintainer and Software Developer, Intern at OpenGenus specializing in Tree Data Structures. She is a Computer Science student at Rajasthan Technical University, Kota.

Ue Kiao is a Japanese Software Developer and has played key role in designing systems like TaoBao, AliPay and many more. She has completed her B. Sc in Mathematics and Computing Science at National Taiwan University and PhD at Tokyo Institute of Technology.

Contributors (16): Benjamin QoChuk, Hrithik Shrivastava, Parth Maniyar, Priyanshi Sharma, Rohit Topi, Amruta U. Koshe, Ayush Sonare, Akshay Gopani, Rashmitha, Manasvi Singh, Sahil Silare, Vaibhav Gupta, Vishnu S Reddy, Kyatham Srikanth, Rupali Kavale, Yash Aggarwal;

All Contributors are associated with OpenGenus.

Published: May 2021 © iq.OpenGenus.org

Table of Contents

Binary Tree

A binary tree is a data structure in which each element links to at most two other elements. It is represented by a starting element from which we can reach the other elements by following the links.

Each element is known as a Node and the starting node of a Binary Tree is known as Root.

In a Binary Tree, every node has at most 2 children that is the left child (left sub-tree) and the right child (right sub-tree). Node of a binary tree will look as follows:

Pointer to Left Child	Data	Pointer to Right Child

You can see that a node consists of three components:

- Pointer to left child node
- Data
- Pointer to right child node

To put this in perspective, think of Linked List data structure where each element links to at most one element. Hence, this is a multi-dimensional version of Linked List.

You can extend this idea to a generalized structure where each node points to at most N other nodes. This structure is known as N-ary Tree. Hence, Binary Tree is an 2-ary Tree.

Suppose there is a binary tree of height "H". The height of root is considered to be 0 as a convention.

Consider this diagram to understand the idea of height of each node:

1

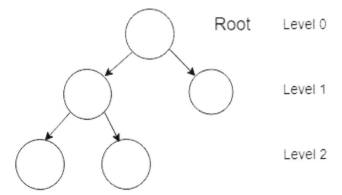

There are four types of binary trees:

- Complete Binary Tree
- Perfect Binary Tree
- Full Binary Tree
- Balanced Binary Tree

Complete Binary Tree : A Binary Tree is complete Binary Tree if all levels are completely filled except the last level and last level should have all nodes as left as possible.

Perfect Binary Tree : A Perfect Binary Tree is a binary tree in which all interior nodes have two children, and all leaves have the same depth that is same level.

Full Binary Tree : A Full Binary Tree is a tree in which every node other than the leaves has two children.

Balanced Binary Tree : A Balanced Binary Tree is a binary tree in which height of the tree is O(log N) where N is the number of nodes.

Basic Operations

A Binary Tree supports the following basic operations:

- Insertion: To insert new element into the Binary Tree
- Deletion: To delete a specific element from a Binary Tree

2

- Search/ Traversal: To go through all elements in a Binary Tree

Insertion operation

Suppose a binary tree is given with few allocated values. As given tree is binary tree, we can insert element wherever we want. Only one property of binary tree should be maintained, and property is that every node can have maximum two children.

We need to insert the new element wherever we find the node whose left or right child is null.

Given (Original Tree) :

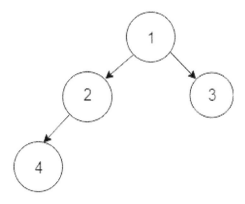

Inserting new element (5) in given tree

Output (New Tree) :

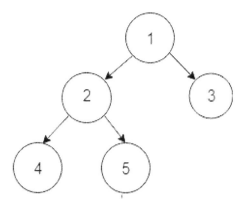

3

Deletion operation

For deletion, first we need to find the element which we want to delete. The basic idea of deletion in a Binary Tree is to replace that element with the right most node (or copy) and then delete the rightmost node.

Given (Original Tree) :

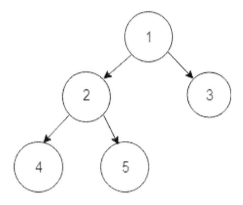

Delete data 3.

Deletion steps :

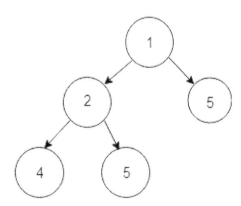

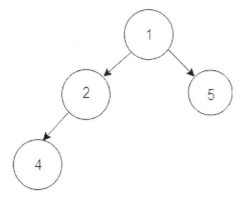

By this way, deletion is done in binary trees.

Time and Space Complexity

Searching : For searching we need to traverse all elements so worst-case time complexity will be O(N) with a space complexity of O(1).

Insertion : Worst case time complexity will be O(N) as it depends on the tree structure. You will understand this well as we move on). The space complexity is O(1).

Deletion : Worst case time complexity will be O(N). The key idea is same as that of Insertion operation which we will understand better in later sections. The space complexity is O(1).

Insight:

With the basic idea of a Binary Tree, you can visualize this as a 2D version of an array where size of each array is limited by a certain value and each array is linked to another array.

Can you visualize this to generalize the idea?

Properties of a Binary Tree

Let us consider that our Binary Tree has N elements. For simplicity, let us assume N is a power of 2.

$N = 2^M$

Visualize the structure of a Balanced Binary Tree. The first level (0) will have 1 node (known as Root). The second level (1) will have 2 nodes. The third level will have 4 nodes which will be children of nodes at second level.

Hence, at level (i), there will be $2^{(i)}$ nodes.

Assume we number the nodes starting from 1 to N in order (top to bottom and left to right). A sample graph will look like this:

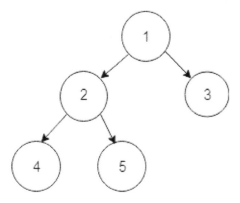

If we assume that such a numbering is done on a Complete Binary Tree (where every node has two child nodes expect the nodes at the last level), then the following points hold:

- Nodes are numbered as 1 to N
- Nodes in level "0" are [1]
- Nodes at level "i" are 2^i to $2^{i+1} - 1$
- Nodes at the last level "H" are 2^H to N
- Children of node "J" will be numbered as "2 x J" and "2 x J + 1"

- Parent of node "J" will be numbered "Floor(J/2)"

These are key points which has two basic applications:

- Represent a Binary Tree as an array where the numbering is used as an index
- Use the numbering to find relationship between nodes. This can solve several challenging problems instantly.

For a Binary Tree, we know the following about the height:

- Height can be N in the worst case where each node has at most 1 child node.
- The minimum height will be "log N". This is the case of a perfectly balanced Binary Tree.
- The ideal case is to maintain the height to be close to "log N".
- Having a height of N, decomposes a Binary Tree to an Array and there are no differences.
- A random Binary Tree achieves the height of "log N" on average.
- There are conditions or modifications of Binary Tree where the height is maintained to be "log N" at all times.
- The height directly impacts the performance of operations like Insert and Delete so it is preferred to keep it as low as possible.

For a Binary Tree of height H, the maximum number of nodes will be $2^{H+1} + 1$ and the minimum number of nodes will be **H**. You can estimate the significant difference between the two cases.

One is linear and the other is exponential.

For a Complete Binary Tree of height H, the number of nodes will be from $2^H + 2$ to $2^{H+1} + 1$.

Insight:

With this, you have a strong idea of the bounds/ limitations of various aspects of a Binary Tree. This will help you in analyzing various algorithms and arrive at the time and space complexity easily.

Implementation of Binary Tree

We will implement a Binary Tree using OOP concepts. We will use a pseudocode which can be converted to the relevant Programming Language (like C++, Java, and Python) easily.

A fundamental component is a Node which is defined as follows:

```
class Node
{
    int data;    // can be any datatype
    Node left;   // Left child node
    Node right;  // Right child node
};
```

When we want to declare a group of data whether of similar or different data types, we use classes in Object Oriented Programming languages like C++ and Java. Other languages has the equivalent to group different datatypes together such as Structures (struct) in C.

Our class is "Node" containing a pointer to left and pointer to right along with a data.

Node left; is pointer to Left child node and stores the address of left child. Similarly, we have right child node. **int data**; declares data of int (Integer) type.

Nodes will be created in Heap memory as Dynamic Memory Allocation shall be used. This relates to malloc function in C and new function in C++ and returns a pointer to the object created. It is important to understand the concepts of stack and heap memory in dynamic allocation.

For linked list, we keep the information of address of the head node. We can access all other nodes from head node using links. In this case, we know the address of the root node, which is must, without this we wot be able to access the tree using links.

9

To declare the Binary tree, we will first need to create a pointer to Node that will store address of root node by : **Node root**. Our tree does not have any data yet, so let us assign our root node as NULL.

```
Node root = NULL;  // Creating an empty tree
```

As seen, we are assigning the left and right cells of nodes as addresses to their child and middle cell is for data. Identity of tree is the address of the root node, and we have declared a pointer to node in which we are storing address of root node. For empty tree, root pointer should be set as NULL.

Consider this rootPtr (root pointer) as a different box pointing towards different nodes in our tree, and for pointing to different nodes we have to pass the address of the nodes.

In the beginning, it is not pointing towards any node and therefore, it has NULL value. As we progressively add more nodes, we will change the address in this rootptr to point towards specific node in which we have to add the data.

```
Node newNode = new Node();  // Creates a new empty node
```

"**Node newNode=new Node();**" Returns the address of newly created node which we are collecting in variable newNode of type 'pointer to Node' because we can access heap memory using pointers. This variable now has structure of a doubly linked list in which data is assigned to data variable of 'newNode' and setting left and right child of 'newNode' as NULL then we are returning address of 'newNode' itself.

If we have the data to be set along with the pointer/ link to Left child node and Right child node, then we can create a new empty node and set the attributes accordingly:

10

```
Node newNode = new Node();   // Creates a new empty node
newNode->Key = key;
newNode->Left = Left_child;
newNode->Right = Right_child;
```

Well, now our tree is empty, we have no data.

Let us insert new data into our tree. For this we will call and define 'Insert' function. Firstly, we will have to call it in our main function as:

```
Node insert(root node, data to be inserted);
```

The key idea will be to:

- Create a new node with the data to be inserted
- Traverse the Binary Tree in order from left to right / top to bottom to find the first empty place
- Insert the new node in the empty place

This will create a Balanced Binary Tree. There are other approaches to insert a new node in a Binary Tree which comes from specific requirements of the problem such as:

- Set new node as the root and move the previous root node accordingly
- Place the new node as the left most or the right most leaf node. This is efficiently as we need not traverse the entire tree and can be done in time proportional to the height of the tree.

We will follow our approach of inserting the new node at the first empty position. The pseudocode of our insertion operation will be:

```
Node InsertNode(Node root, int data)
{
    // If the tree is empty, create a new node as Root
    if (root == NULL)
    {
        root = NewNode(data);
        return root;
    }

    // Find the first empty place
    // where node can be inserted
    // Queue of Nodes to keep track of nodes to be processed
    queue<Node> q;
    q.push(root);

    while (q is not empty)
    {
        Node temp = q.front();
        q.pop();

        // If left node is not NULL, put it in queue
        if (temp->left != NULL)
            q.push(temp->left);
        // If left node is NULL, empty space have been found
        else
        {
            temp->left = NewNode(data);
            return root;
        }

        // If right node is not NULL, put it in queue
        if (temp->right != NULL)
            q.push(temp->right);
        // If right node is NULL, empty space have been found
        else
        {
            temp->right = NewNode(data);
            return root;
        }
    }
}
```

Go through the pseudocode and you will get the complete idea.

We used a NewNode() function to create a new node with a given value which can be implemented as follows:

```
Node NewNode(int key)
{
    Node newNode = new Node;
    newNode->key = key;
    newNode->left = NULL;
    newNode->right = NULL;
    return newNode;
};
```

Following images clarify the process of inserting a new data in a Binary Tree:

Given (Original Tree) :

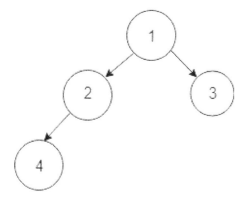

Inserting new element (5) in given tree

Output (New Tree) :

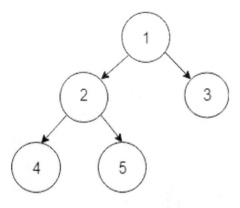

You can easily expand the Insert function to perform the traversal of a Binary Tree or search for a specific element. Try it. We will present this part following the deletion operation.

Deletion Operation

There are multiple approaches to delete a node from a Binary Tree. Some of the common approaches are:

- Delete the concerned node and place a leaf node (mainly, the rightmost left node) in its place.
- Delete the concerned node, place the right or left child node in its place and delete the original placed node accordingly.

We will take the second approach. Both approaches are equivalent in terms of performance, but the second approach is preferred as it maintains the balanced nature of the original Binary Tree.

Consider the following Binary Tree:

14

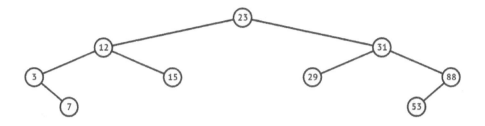

There are 3 possible cases for removing the node from the tree which are as follows:

- Case 1: Remove leaf node
- Case 2: Remove node with one child node only
- Case 3: Remove node with two child nodes

The idea behind each of the three cases are as follows:

- Removing the leaf node is the easiest case of the three. We just have to remove the node which does not have any child. In our tree, leaf nodes are- 8, 12, 17, 25
- If the removed node has one child (either left or right). After deleting the node we just have to point the address of parent node to the child node of the deleted one. for example, in above tree, nodes 88 and 3 have a single node. If we want to remove node 88 then we have to point parent node of 53 to 31 and make right node of 31 as 53.
- Removing the node with 2 children. If our node has 2 children then first find out the successor or predecessor of that node, then replace that node with successor or predecessor node. For eg if want to removes node 12, then first anyone of the successor or predecessor, let us find predecessor to 12, which is 7 then replace 12 with 7. Now, 7 has 15 and 3 as its children. As we can choose anyone of the successor or predecessor, we could have 2 binary tree representations after deletion of a node. For this case we first have to define predecessor and successor of a node.

The pseudocode of our deletion operation is as follows:

15

```
Node Remove(root node, key to be deleted)
{
    // Find the node to be deleted
    node = search(root node, key to be deleted)

    // The given node is not found
    if (node == NULL)
        return NULL;

    // Target node is found
    if (node->Key == key)
    {
        // If the node is a leaf node
        if (node->Left == NULL && node->Right == NULL)
            node = NULL;

        // The node have only one child at right
        else if (node->Left == NULL && node->Right != NULL)
        {
            // The only child will be connected to the parent of
node directly
            node->Right->Parent = node->Parent;
            // Bypass node
            node = node->Right;
        }
        // The node have only one child at left
        else if (node->Left != NULL && node->Right == NULL)
        {
            // The only child will be connected to the parent of
node directly
            node->Left->Parent = node->Parent;
            // Bypass node
            node = node->Left;
        }

        // The node have two children (left and right)
        else
        {
            // Get key of right child node
            int rightKey = node->Right->key;

            // Replace node's key with right child node's key
            node->Key = rightKey;
            // Delete the original right child node
```

16

```
          node->Right = Remove(node->Right, rightKey);
        }
    }
// Return the updated Binary Tree
return node;
}
```

In this, we do only one traversal:

- At first, we traverse till the node to be deleted
- Following this, we traverse through the remaining nodes to replace the deleted node

Note that from the point of structure of the Binary Tree, only one leaf node is deleted so the balanced nature of the tree is maintained.

The search() function finds the node to be deleted and returns a link to that node. We can search the node using a search utility which will be similar to our insertion function.

For our insertion function, we took an iterative approach. For our search function, we will take a recursive approach with the same basic idea so that you get the idea clearly and get flexible with both approaches.

The algorithmic steps for search are as follows:

- If current node matches the data to be searched, return the current node.
- If node not found, search in the right sub-tree and left sub-tree.

The pseudocode of our search function is as follows:

```
Node Search(Node node, int key)
{
```

17

```
    // The given key is not found
    if (node == NULL)
        return NULL;

    // The given key is found
    else if(node->key == key)
        return node;

    // Search right side of Binary Tree
    Node right = Search(node->right, key)

    // If node not found in right side
    if(right == NULL)
        return Search(node->left, key)
    else
        return right
}
```

With this, you have the implementation idea of the three basic operations of a Binary Tree:

- Insertion
- Deletion
- Search

Insight:

The details we have covered is the most common implementation strategy. The main disadvantage is the use of NULL. This is because NULL is considered as a special case and for each algorithm, we need to consider NULL along with other conditions. Hence, NULL is an edge case.

NULL condition has been the cause of several runtime bugs in production system.

Hence, it is advised to not use NULL in implementations. The use of the previous implementation is good for non-production and not highly critical systems and for use case like Competitive Programming. If you are a professional programmer and

18

planning to use Binary Tree to solve a specific problem, consider using the better version without NULL which we will present next.

Implementation of Binary Tree with no NULL

To illustrate the benefit of not using NULL, we will use a variant of Binary Tree that is Binary Search Tree. In Binary Search Tree (BST), there is only one extra property which is followed by every node:

- Key of current node be K1
- Then, key of left child node of the current node is less (<) than K1
- And key of right child node of the current node is greater (>) than K1

Consider the following Binary Search Tree (BST):

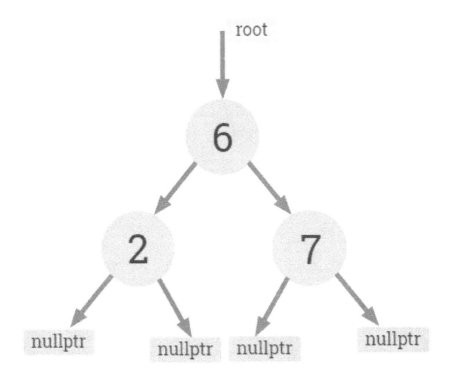

The usual implementation

In the implementation of Binary Search Tree, each node contains a left pointer, a right pointer, and a key element. The root pointer points to the topmost node in the tree. The left and right pointers recursively point to smaller subtrees on either side. A null pointer represents a binary tree with no elements (the empty tree).

Use of NULL

NULL is the null pointer literal used in C and sometimes even in C++. It defines a null pointer value. In the BST, they are used to indicate the absence of a node.

The NULL values are a useful implementation feature but in reality, it is advised to avoid using NULL in designing software as it increases the number of edge cases and needs to be handled separately. The prominent reason for this is due to the fact that NULL represents both the value 0 and a null pointer literal. Thus, the usage is not type safe.

Placeholder nodes

In our implementation, the placeholder nodes (instead of NULL) indicate the absence of a node. Since we will be using nodes themselves to indicate absence of nodes, we need a way to differentiate them.

We could ideally assume that their key values are negative infinity or positive infinity but we cannot really use infinity, so we use the value of macros INT_MIN and INT_MAX defined in header <climits> for the left and right nodes respectively. Similar constants are available in all Programming Languages.

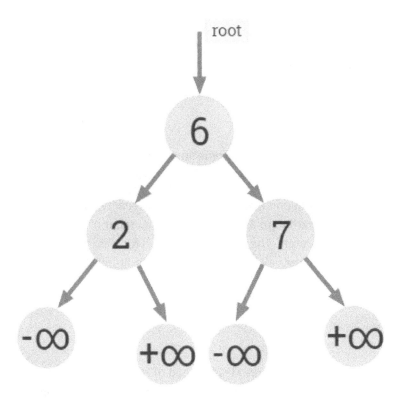

The reason of using INT_MIN and INT_MAX values is because we assume that they are small enough and large enough respectively to not be used in other nodes.

Checking for placeholder nodes

We need a way to determine if a node is a placeholder node.

We define a function isPlaceholderNode() to do that. This is analogous to checking for NULL value in the usual implementation.

```
// a placeholder node is characterized by its key value
// returns true or false depending on whether or
// not the node is a placeholder node
bool isPlaceholderNode(node* n)
{
```

22

```
    return n->key == INT_MAX || n->key == INT_MIN;
}
```

BST nodes

The node contains an integer key and two pointers left and right. This is similar to a Conventional binary tree.

```
Node
{
    int key;
    Node left;
    Node right;

    // constructor
    node(int key)
    {
        key = key, left = NULL, right = NULL
    }
};
```

Due to this, there is a constructor and member initialization is done as well.

Creating a BST node

We will use a function that returns a pointer to a newly created node. The node would have two placeholder nodes (in place of NULL).

```
Node getNewNode(int key)
{
    Node t;
    t = new node(key);  // node
    t->left = new node(INT_MIN);  // placeholder node
    t->right = new node(INT_MAX);  // placeholder node
    return t;
}
```

23

BST operations

Inserting a node

A new node is always inserted as a leaf node.

If the tree is empty, we insert the node as root. If the tree is non-empty then to insert a node, we start from the root node and if the node to insert is less than the root, we go to left child, otherwise we go to the right child of the root. We continue this traversal until we find a placeholder node (or a leaf node) where we cannot go any further. We then insert the node as a left or right child of the leaf node depending on whether the node is less or greater than the leaf node.

Note that we have to replace the placeholder node for insertion. i.e., delete the placeholder node first and then insert a new node.

```
Node insertNode(Node root, int key)
{
    // insert the node by first 'deleting' the placeholder node
    if (isPlaceholderNode(root)){
        delete(root);
        return getNewNode(key);
    }

    // to determine a place to insert the node, traverse left
    if (key < root->key)
    {
        root->left = insertNode(root->left, key);
    }
    else
    { // or traverse right
        root->right = insertNode(root->right, key);
    }
    return root;
}
```

Deleting a node

Deleting a node has several cases, depending on the type of node we want to delete. For convenience, let us assume the node to be deleted is N.

24

N is a leaf node (i.e., has no child nodes) - In this case we just delete the node.

node to delete has one child node - In this case we cannot directly delete the node. So, we first promote its child node to its place here if the node to be deleted is a left child of the parent, then we connect the left pointer of the parent (of the deleted node) to the single child. Otherwise, if the node to be deleted is a right child of the parent, then we connect the right pointer of the parent (of the deleted node) to single child.

node to delete has two child nodes - In this case the node N to be deleted has two sub-trees. here we need to find the minimum node in the right sub-tree of node N and then replace it with N. In the code we use minValueNode(root->right) to find the minimum value in the right sub-tree.

```
Node deleteNode(Node root, int key)
{
    // node not found
    if(isPlaceholderNode(root))
    {
        return root;
    }

    if(key < (root->key))
    { // traverse left
        root->left = deleteNode((root->left), key);
    }
    else if (key > (root->key))
    { // traverse right
        root->right = deleteNode((root->right), key);
    }
    else
    {   // node found

        // case: node has zero / one right child node
        if (isPlaceholderNode(root->left))
        {
            node *temp = root->right;
            delete(root);
            return temp;
```

25

```
        }
        // case: node has one left-child node
        else if (isPlaceholderNode(root->right))
        {
                node *temp = root->left;
                delete(root);
                return temp;
        }

        // case: node with both children
        //       get successor and then delete the node
        node* temp = minValueNode(root->right);

        // Copy the inorder successor's content to this node
        root->key = temp->key;

        // Delete the inorder successor
        root->right = deleteNode(root->right, temp->key);
    }
    return root;
}
```

The minValueNode() function is implemented as below

```
Node minValueNode(Node root)
{
    Node current = root;

    // search the leftmost tree
    while (!isPlaceholderNode(current)
            && !isPlaceholderNode(current->left))
    {
        current = current->left;
    }
    return current;
}
```

Searching for a key

26

Suppose we are searching for a key K. When we are at some node. If this node has the key that we are searching for, then the search is over, and we return true. Otherwise, the key at the current node is either smaller or greater than K.

By using the BST property, we know for any root, its left sub-tree will have key values less than that of root, and its right sub-tree will have key values greater than that of root, thus we decide to traverse left or right.

```
boolean search(Node root, int key)
{
    if(!isPlaceholderNode(root))
    {
        if(root->key == key)
        {  // found
            return true;
        }
        else
        {
            if(root->key > key)
            {
                // check in left sub-tree
                return search(root->left, key);
            }
            else
            {
                // check in right sub-tree
                return search(root->right, key);
            }
        }
    }
    else
    {
        // empty sub-tree
        return false;
    }
}
```

Inorder traversal

To print the tree, we use the inorder traversal in this implementation. Inorder traversal always produces the keys in a sorted order. The reason for this is due to

27

the order of visits. For any root, the left sub-tree of the root is visited first then the root is visited and then finally the right sub-tree is visited.

In the function given below we first check if the pointer root is pointing to a placeholder node. If it is then, it means that the sub-tree is empty, in which case it returns, else it recursively traverses the left sub-tree and then prints the root and then recursively traverses the right subtree.

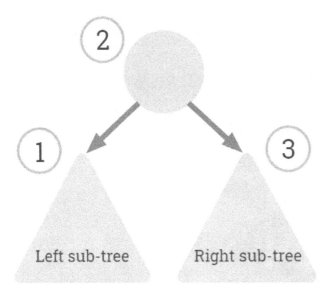

The pseudocode is as follows:

```
void inorder(Node root)
{
    if (!isPlaceholderNode(root))
    {
        // print left first, then root and then right
        inorder(root->left);
        print (root->key);
        inorder(root->right);
    }
}
```

28

With this, you have the complete idea of using Placeholder nodes to avoid use of NULL. You can use the same idea of placeholder nodes in other variants of Binary Tree.

Insight:

Implementing Data Structures without the use of NULL is a standard practice for producing high quality code but is not commonly known. You know this technique now and this puts you at an advantage along with top 0.1% of Programmers.

You may try it apply this idea for the problems we will explore and make yourself comfortable with this technique.

Intuitive View of a Binary Tree

A Binary Tree is a more powerful data structure than you might imagine it to be. Each node of a Binary Tree leads to two paths or options. If the Binary Tree is complete and balanced, with each move, we are reducing the search space by a factor of 2.

The most common approach is to use this property to split smaller elements on the left side and larger elements on the right side. This results in a worst-case search time complexity of O(log N). To understand the importance, we are checking only logN elements to find a specific element among N elements and are sure that the other elements need not be checked.

It is important to note that we split the data with respect to other attributes as well like position in space. The real position will be clear as we go through this book.

We will see in the last section of this book on how this property is used in various use cases like Binary Tree is used in Excel sheets. With this knowledge, you will be able to apply Binary Tree in difficult problems which might seem to be unrelated at first sight.

As we reduce the length of a distinct path from root to leaf to logN, we have reduced the size of the search space or dataset exponentially. In fact, N is exponential when compared to logN.

Traversing a Binary Tree (Preorder, Postorder, Inorder)

In linear data structures like arrays and linked lists, we could traverse them in one way but in tree data structures like binary tree, we could traverse them in different ways. like:

- Depth First traversals
- Breadth First traversals

Depth first traversals of Binary tree:

- Inorder traversal
- Preorder traversal
- Postorder traversal

We will learn about inorder, preorder and postorder and their use. These three types of traversals generally used in different types of binary tree.

In summary:

- Inorder: left, root, right
- Preorder: root, left, right
- Postorder: left, right, root

Inorder Traversal

In Inorder traversal we traverse from left-root-right.

In this traversal. left subtree visited first then the root and later the right subtree.

Remember that every node may represent a subtree itself and hence, be the root of that subtree. Every node needs to follow the rules.

Algorithm

- Until all nodes are traversed

31

- Recursively Traverse the left subtree
- Visit the Root.
- Recursively Traverse the right subtree.

Example of inorder traversal

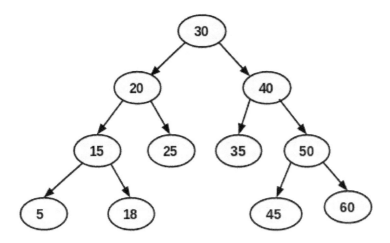

We start recursive call from 30 (root) then move to 20 (20 also have sub tree so apply in order on it), 15 and 5.

5 have no child .so print 5 then move to it's parent node which is 15 print and then move to 15's right node which is 18.

18 have no child print 18 and move to 20. Print 20 then move it right node which is 25 .25 have no subtree so print 25.

Print root node 30 .

Now recursively traverse to right subtree of root node, so move to 40. 40 have subtree so traverse to left subtree of 40.

Left subtree of 40 have only one node which is 35. 35 has no further subtree so print 35. Move to 40 and print 40.

Traverse to right subtree of 40. Move to 50 now and we have a subtree so traverse to left subtree of 50. Move to 45 , 45 have no further subtree so print 45.

32

Move to 50 and print 50. now traverse to right subtree of 50 hence move to 60 and print 60.

Our final output is {5 , 15 , 18 , 20 , 25 , 30 , 35 , 40 , 45 , 50 , 60}

Application of inorder traversal

In-order traversal is used to retrieve data of binary search tree in sorted order.

```
def Inorder(root):
    if root:
        Inorder(root.left)
        print(root.key,end=" ")
        Inorder(root.right)
```

Preorder Traversal

In Preorder traversal we traverse from root-left-right.

In this traversal root visited first then the left subtree and later the right subtree. Remember that every node may represent a subtree itself and needs to follow the rules.

Algorithm of preorder traversal

- Until all nodes are traversed
- Visit the Root
- Recursively Traverse the left subtree
- Recursively Traverse the right subtree

Example of preorder traversal

Consider the following Binary Tree:

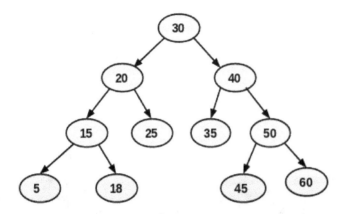

Start with root node 30. Print 30 as it is the root and recursively traverse the left subtree.

Next node is 20. Now 20 has a subtree so print 20 as it is the root of the current subtree and traverse to left subtree of 20 .

Next node is 15 and 15 has a subtree so print 15 and traverse to left subtree of 15.

5 is next node and 5 have no subtree so print 5 and traverse to right subtree of 15.

Next node is 18 and 18 have no child so print 18 as it is the root of a subtree with only one node and traverse to right subtree of 20.

25 is right subtree of 20. 25 has no child so print 25 and start traverse to right subtree of 30.

Next node is 40. Node 40 have subtree so print 40 and then traverse to left subtree of 40.

Next node is 35. 35 have no subtree so print 35 and then traverse to right subtree of 40.

Next node is 50. 50 has a subtree so print 50 and traverse to left subtree of 50.

Next node is 45. 45 have no subtree so print 45 and then print 60 (right subtree) of 50.

Our final output is {30 , 20 , 15 , 5 , 18 , 25 , 40 , 35 , 50 , 45 , 60}

Application of preorder traversal

34

Preorder traversal is used to create a copy of the tree.

Preorder traversal is also used to get prefix expression of an expression tree.

Implementation of preorder traversal in Python:

```python
def Preorder(root) :
    if root :
        print(root.key,end=" ")
        Preorder(root.left)
        Preorder(root.right)
```

Postorder Traversal

In Preorder traversal, we traverse from left-right-root.

In this traversal, left subtree visited first then the right subtree and later the root.

Remember that every node may represent a subtree itself and must follow the rules as with the previous two traversal techniques.

Algorithm of postorder traversal

- Until all nodes are traversed
- Recursively Traverse the left subtree
- Recursively Traverse the right subtree.
- Visit the Root.

Example of postorder traversal

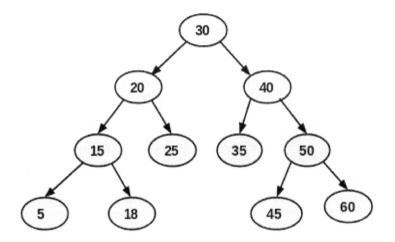

We start from 30, and following Post-order traversal, we first visit the left subtree 20. 20 is also traversed post-order.

15 is left subtree of 20. 15 is also traversed post order.

5 is left subtree of 15. 5 have no subtree so print 5 and traverse to right subtree of 15 .

18 is right subtree of 15. 18 have no subtree so print 18 and then print 15. Post order traversal for 15 is finished.

Next move to right subtree of 20.

25 is right subtree of 20. 25 has no subtree so print 25 and then print 20. Post order traversal for 20 is finished.

Next visit the right subtree of 30 which is 40. 40 is also traversed post-order (40 has a subtree).

35 is left subtree of 40. 35 have no more sub-tree so print 35 and traverse to right subtree of 40.

50 is right subtree of 40. 50 should also traversed post order.

45 is left subtree of 50. 45 have no more sub-tree so print 45 and then print 60 which is right subtree of 50.

Next print 50. Post order traversal for 50 is finished.

Now print 40 and post order traversal for 40 is finished.

36

Print 30. Post order traversal for 30 is finished.

Our final output is {5 , 18 , 15 , 25 , 20 , 35 , 45 , 60 , 50 , 40 , 30}

Application of postorder traversal

- Postorder traversal is used to delete the tree.
- Postorder traversal is also used to get the postfix expression of an expression tree.

Implementation of postorder traversal

```
def Postorder(root) :
    if root :
        Postorder(root.left)
        Postorder(root.right)
        print(root.key,end=" ")
```

Summary

Time complexity for all three traversals (Inorder, Preorder, Postorder) is O(N) so it depends on the problem which traversal should be chosen. N is the number of nodes/ elements in the Binary Tree.

In summary:

- Inorder: left, root, right
- Preorder: root, left, right
- Postorder: left, right, root

Insight:

The traversal techniques we explored are standard techniques that are used widely. A reasonable traversal technique shall take O(N) time complexity by the space complexity may vary from O(1) to O(N). This does not restrict you to other combinations of traversals which we explore in further chapters.

Can you figure out other types of traversal at this point?

Convert Inorder + Preorder to Binary Tree (+ other combinations)

In this problem, we will construct a Binary Tree provided we have the inorder traversal and preorder traversal of our destination Binary Tree. We present two approaches to Construct Binary Tree from Inorder and Preorder traversal.

We start with background information on constructing Binary Tree from a given traversal or a set of traversals.

Introduction

Why we cannot use only Inorder traversal to construct Binary Tree?

In order to construct a unique binary tree, we cannot rely only on the Inorder Traversal. With only inorder traversal of the binary tree and no more information we may find a binary tree but not a unique binary tree.

From the inorder traversal, we could pick possibly more than one node as root node. If the tree does not have to be balanced, then we could potentially pick any node as root node.

Example:

Inorder Traversal : [**1,2,3,4,5,6,7,8**]

We can form non-balanced tree by having the left most element (1 as the root of the entire Binary Tree) as root node of concerned sub-tree:

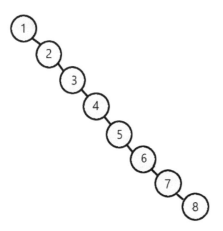

The pre-order traversal of this tree would be [**1,2,3,4,5,6,7,8**]

Now, for the same tree we can consider node 4 as root node.

It would look something like this:

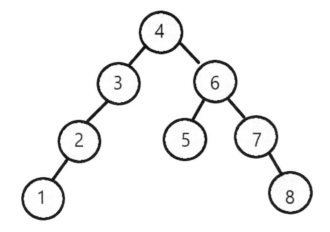

It will have pre-order traversal as [**4,3,2,1,6,5,7,8**]

Since both the above trees generate the same in-order traversal but different pre-order traversal, there is no guarantee for a single, unique binary tree to be formed from the Inorder traversal. Hence, we need additional traversal information for the Binary Tree to be unique.

We have 3 types of Traversals so you can imagine that we have 7 combinations and to figure out if we can construct a Binary Tree for a given combination and for a new traversal technique, you need insights in this direction.

Let us understand this point in an intuitive way

Can we construct Binary Tree from Inorder traversal only? and what about other combinations?

Yes, we can construct a Binary Tree from Inorder traversal only but we cannot construct an unique Binary Tree from a single traversal (inorder or preorder or postorder). This is because from a given traversal, we have the following information:

- Inorder -> We know the leftmost and rightmost node in Binary Tree
- Preorder -> We know the root node of the Binary Tree for sure
- Postorder -> We know the root node of the Binary Tree for sure

The three traversals in summary:

- Inorder: left, root, right
- Preorder: root, left, right
- Postorder: left, right, root

The problems are as follows:

- **Problem with Inorder**

With Inorder traversal, we know the leftmost and rightmost node in the Binary Tree, but we do not know the root of the Binary Tree.

Hence, any node (including the leftmost or the rightmost node) can be the root of the Binary Tree.

If we consider the leftmost node as the root node, then we get a right skewed Binary Tree.

If we consider the rightmost node as the root node, then we get a left skewed Binary Tree.

The problem exists from every subtree of the Binary Tree. We have no information about the root node.

Problem with Preorder

With Preorder traversal, we know the root of the Binary Tree for sure, but we do not know the leftmost or rightmost node of the Binary Tree.

Consider the case when we can have no right sub-tree from the root. Then, the traversal will go into the left subtree directly and the last node will be in the left sub-tree and is not the rightmost node.

Therefore, we cannot create a unique Binary Tree using Preorder.

Problem with Postorder

With Postorder traversal, we know the root of the Binary Tree for sure, but we do not know the leftmost or rightmost node of the Binary Tree.

Consider the case when we can have no left sub-tree from the root. Then, the traversal will go into the right sub-tree directly and the first node will be in the right sub-tree and is not the leftmost node.

Therefore, we cannot create a unique Binary Tree using Postorder.

Which combinations will work?

42

To construct a unique Binary Tree, we need to know the exact nodes that are:

- Root
- Leftmost node
- Rightmost node

Preorder and Postorder traversal give us information about the root node.

Inorder traversal give us information about the leftmost and rightmost node.

Hence, if we take any two traversals: one being Inorder and the order from Preorder or Postorder, we can create a unique Binary Tree.

Note: We cannot create a Unique Binary Tree from the combination of Preorder and Postorder traversal as we have the information of the root only.

Hence, combinations from which we can create a unique Binary Tree are:

- Inorder + Postorder
- Inorder + Preorder

Combinations from which we cannot create a unique Binary Tree are:

- Inorder
- Postorder
- Preorder
- Preorder + Postorder

Inorder + Preorder to Binary Tree

Let us construct tree from given Inorder and Preorder Traversals.

Let us assume that the Inorder Sequence is [**4, 2, 5, 1, 6, 3**]

Preorder Traversal is [**1, 2, 4, 5, 3, 6**]

Now from the preorder sequence, we know that the leftmost element is the root of the tree. That is node **1 is the root of the tree**. Now, we will search node 1 in inorder sequence and find elements on the left side of root node and those to the right.

From above, we know that node 1 is the root node and node 4, 2, 5 are on the left whereas node 6 and 3 on right. Based on this, we can find the parts in the preorder traversal that corresponds to the left sub-tree and the right sub-tree.

We need to follow the same procedure for the left sub-tree and right sub-tree.

Eventually, we will get this:

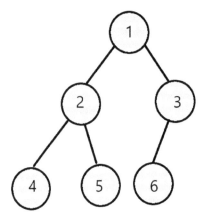

Approach 1

Algorithm:

- Pick the first element from the preorder and then increment the preorder index variable for next element in next recursive call.
- Create new tree node with data as picked element.
- Find that element index in Inorder traversal.
- Call function again for elements before index of that element and build the left subtree of node.
- Call the function for elements after that element index for right subtree.
- Return the root node.

Now we have the helper function to help us find the index value in array. We will assume the value is present in the inorder traversal.

44

```
int helper(char arr[], int start, int end, int value)
{
    int i;
    for (i = start; i <= end; i++)
    {
        if (arr[i] == value)
            return i;
    }
}
```

Now we define the function maketree, this will be our recursive function to construct the binary tree of size length from Inorder traversal and preorder traversal.

- First, we pick the current node from Preorder traversal using the preIndex and increment preIndex
- If that node has no children, then we will return
- Else we find the index of this node in Inorder traversal
- Using the index in the Inorder traversal, we will construct the left and right subtree.

Following is the implementation of maketree function:

```
node* maketree(int in[], int pre[], int istart, int iend)
{
    static int preIndex = 0;
    if (istart > iend)
        return NULL;
    node* finNode = newNode(pre[preIndex++]);
    if (istart == iend)
        return finNode;
    int iIndex = helper(in, istart, iend, finNode->data);
    finNode->left = maketree(in, pre, istart, iIndex - 1);
    finNode->right = maketree(in, pre, iIndex + 1, iend);

    return finNode;
}
```

45

Time complexity will be **O(N²)**

Approach 2:

We can use hashmap for the above problem as well. We can store the indexes of the inorder traversal in hash table and then we can perform our search in O(1) time in average.

- We start by picking the current node from preorder traversal using the preIndex and increment it
- If the node has no children, then we will return
- Else we will find the index of this node in Inorder traversal
- Use the index in Inorder traversal and we will construct the left and right subtree

Following is the implementation of maketree function:

```
struct Node* maketree(int in[], int pre[], int istart,
                      int iend, unordered_map<int, int>& mp)
{
    static int preIndex = 0;
    if (istart > iend)
        return NULL;
    int curr = pre[preIndex++];
    struct Node* finNode = newNode(curr);
    if (istart == iend)
        return finNode;
    int inIndex = mp[curr];
    finNode->left = maketree(in, pre, istart, inIndex - 1, mp);
    finNode->right = maketree(in, pre, inIndex + 1, iend, mp);
    return finNode;
}
```

Time complexity: **O(N)**

46

Note: The time complexity is same to get the traversal and to generate the Binary Tree from the traversal.

Construction of the binary tree from Inorder and Postorder Traversal

Example:

Inorder Traversal: **[4, 2, 5, 1, 3]**

Postorder Traversal: **[4, 5, 2, 3, 1]**

Now from the postorder traversal we can see the right most element, node 1 is the root node. From Inorder traversal we can see that node 3 is on right of root node 1, and others on left. In similar fashion, we end up with tree:

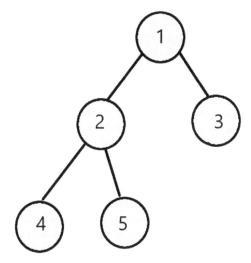

For the construction of the binary tree from the inorder traversal and postorder traversal, we can use the same concept as used in above approach (inorder + preorder) to find our tree.

By using both recursion and hashmap, we will be able to re-construct our tree from the traversals.

We already know which combination will give us a unique Binary Tree.

47

Another point to note is that if we have a special knowledge of the Binary Tree like it is a Balanced Binary Tree or a Binary Search Tree, then we can recreate the original Binary Tree from just one traversal.

For example, if we know that the Binary Tree is balanced and is complete tree, then the middle element will be the root and hence, we can recreate the original tree from a given inorder traversal.

Insight:

The time complexity to do a traversal is same as the time complexity to recreate the Binary Tree from a given traversal or a set of traversals. This brings in the idea that even if we do not have any information about the Binary Tree, we can store the entire information in at most 2 traversals (or linear arrangement of the elements).

See Binary Tree is a 2D data structure and the information can be stored in 2 1D data structures (array or list). **Think over this point.**

Find height or depth of a Binary Tree

The length of the longest path from the root of a binary tree to a leaf node is the height of the binary tree. It is, also, known as depth of a binary tree.

The height of the root is the height of the tree.

The depth of a node is the length of the path to its root.

We need to find the number of edges between the Binary Tree's root and its furthest leaf to compute the height of tree.

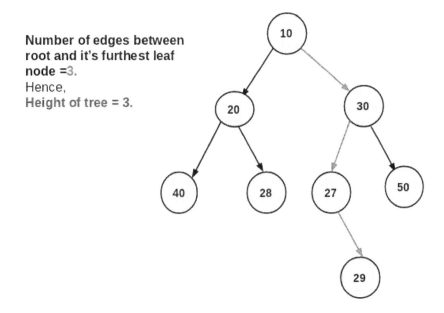

Number of edges between root and it's furthest leaf node =3.
Hence,
Height of tree = 3.

In above example number of edges between root and furthest leaf is 3. Hence, height of tree is 3.

We will compute the height of tree by recursively compute the height of left and right subtree and then get the maximum of the two values as the height of tree.

Steps to find height of binary tree

Following are the steps to compute the height of a binary tree:

49

- If tree is empty, then height of tree is 0.
- If tree is not empty, start from the root
- Find the maximum depth of left sub-tree recursively.
- Find the maximum depth of right sub-tree recursively.
- Maximum depth of the two is (left and right subtree) the height of binary tree.

Example :

Number of edges between root and it's furthest leaf node =2.
Hence,
Height of tree = 2.

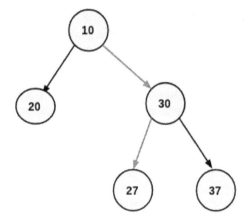

Start with root node , and recursively find maximum depth of left and right subtree.

Our next node is 20 . 20 is leaf node and as leaf node have no child, height of left subtree is 1.

Now recursively traverse to right subtree, next node is 30. 30 have both left and right node .

First traverse to left side so next node is 27. 27 is leaf node leaf and have no child. left subtree of 30 will return 1.

Next apply same process for right subtree of node 30 . It will return 1.

Height of node 30 is 1 . Number of edges between root to node 30 is 1.

So, total height of right subtree is 1+1=2.

The height of right subtree is greater than left subtree so height of tree = height of right subtree = 2.

50

Pseudocode

Following is the pseudocode of the algorithm:

```
int height(Node root)
// return the height of tree
{
        if(root == null)
                return -1;
        else
        {
                int left=height(root.left);
                int right=height(root.right);

                if (left > right)
                        return left+1;
                else
                        return right+1;
        }
}
```

Complexity

Time complexity : O(N) where N is the number of nodes in the Binary Tree.

It is linear as we are traversing all nodes of Binary Tree recursively and maintaining the height. So, the time complexity is O(N) where N is the number of nodes in the tree.

This can be solved using a standard graph traversal technique like Breadth First Search and Depth First Search as well. Modification of inorder, preorder and postorder traversals make the process of calculating the height of Binary Tree.

Insight:

This is a standard problem but is used as a sub-routine in solve some of the challenging Binary Tree problems. This is a standard definition and approaches to find defined values are important.

Can you imagine how height of a node may be useful?

Find Level of each node from root node

We will discuss how to find the level of each node in a Binary Tree. We will use a variant of Breadth First Search (BFS) and in the process, you will understand the idea behind this algorithm BFS. This diagram illustrates the idea of level:

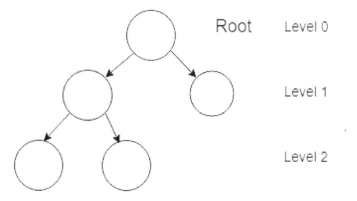

- Root is always at level 0 (by convention)
- The child nodes of the root node are at level 1 and so on.

There are a few terminologies that you should know before going to the algorithm:

- Root: The node from which we start our breadth first search traversal is called the root or source node.
- Level: The level of a node is defined by 1 + the number of connections between the node and the root.
- Leaf Node: Any node whose left and right child are null is called the leaf node of the graph.

Hence, level of a node is the length of the path from the root node to that node. As the length of path from root node to root node is 0, level of root node is 0.

Algorithm

- Step 1 : Set level of root node as 1.

53

- Step 2 : Pop the first element in the queue and enqueue all the nodes which are directly connected to the popped element.
- Step 3 : Set the level of all the element which are enqueued in the previous Step to 1 more than element popped in the second step.
- Step 4 : Repeat process 2 and 3 until the queue is empty.
- Step 5 : Exit

Explanation

This algorithm follows breadth first search algorithm at the core.

After the graph has been created, we will set the level of the root node in the level vector as 0 and then apply the breadth first search.

In this algorithm we will pop the first element of the queue and set the level of all of connected nodes as 1 more than the element popped from the queue and simultaneously push the connected nodes in the queue.

We just keep repeating this process explained in until queue is empty.

At the end we will have level of all the nodes in the graph with respect to the root node.

Example

The graph shown below is a 3-level graph (level 0 , 1 and 2) and we can find the level of each node in the graph using Breadth First Search .

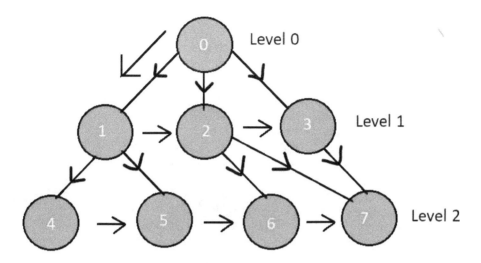

We will also create a level vector which stores the level of each node .

In the process, first we will set the level of node 0 (root node) as 0 and enqueue it in the queue.

Now , we will pop the first element of the queue (which is 0 initially) and push all the neighboring nodes (2 and 3) in the queue and set level of all the neighboring nodes 1 more than the node element we just popped from the queue.

Now we have node 1 , 2 and 3 in the queue , now we will repeat the same process explained in the above step , first we will deque the first element (node 1) and set the level of neighboring nodes (node 4 and 5) to more than the first node which we just dequeued.

We will repeat the same process with nodes 2 and 3.

At last, we will have 4 , 5 , 6 and 7 nodes in the queue so will just pop each element because there are no neighboring elements to these elements which are unvisited.

55

Now, we will just print the level vector which describes the level of each node.

```
vector levelOrderTraversal(root , graph[] , n)
{
    // creating a level vector for storing the data
    // of level of each node compared to the root node
    vector<int> level(n) ;
    queue<Node> q ;

    // initially pushing the root in the queue and
    // setting it iss level as 0
    q.push(root) ;
    level[root] = 0 ;

    // continuing this process uptil queue is empty
    while( !q.empty() )
    {

        Node x = q.front() ;
        q.pop() ;

        // popping the first element and setting up
        // the level of all the connected
        // nodes to the current node
        for( node in [x.left_child, x.right_child])
        {
            // setting up the level of node to 1
            // more than the current level
            q.push(node) ;
            level[node] = level[x] + 1 ;
        }
    }
    return level ;

}
```

Complexity Analysis

- Time Complexity: O(N)

In BFS traversal every node is visited only once, so Time Complexity is O(N) where N is the number of nodes in the Binary Tree.

- Space Complexity: O(N).

The space is required to store the nodes in a queue and also their level in the array.

Insight:

The technique we explored is also known as Level Order traversal and is a traversal technique alternative to Inorder, Preorder and Postorder traversal. Find the level of a node is the direct application of this technique but it goes beyond this as we will see in further problems.

Diameter of a Binary Tree

In this problem, we are given input as the reference to the root of a binary tree. We need to find the diameter of the tree. We solve this using two approaches:

- Approach 1: Using recursion
- Approach 3: Using DFS in a naïve way
- Approach 2: Using DFS efficiently

Diameter of a Tree: It is defined as the number of nodes on the longest path between 2 nodes. This path may or may not pass through the root of the tree. This path includes two leaf nodes. It is also known as the width of a tree.

Note in a Binary Tree, we consider edges are bidirectional as in a graph to keep the definition of Diameter valid for Binary Tree. Each node has a degree of 2 or less.

There can be two possibilities for the longest path of a tree

- It passes through the root.
- It does not pass through the root.

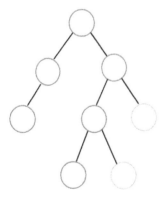
Longest path passes through the root

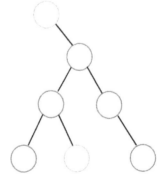
Longest path doesn't pass through the root

In the first example, the diameter is 6, and for the second one, diameter is 5.

There can be more than one longest path, but the diameter will always be maximum.

This problem can be solved with various methods:

Approach 1: Use recursion

We use recursion to calculate the height of a subtree and the diameter. So, we make a recursive function that is diameter(node)

We can consider that the diameter up to any given node will be the sum of the height of its left and right subtrees and 1.

Hence,

Diameter = Left subtree height + Right subtree height + 1.

- If the node that is passed in the recursive function is null, then return zero.
- Calculate the height of the left subtree.
- Calculate the height of the right subtree.
- Calculate the diameter of the left subtree using recursive call till node becomes null.
- Calculate diameter of the right subtree using recursion till node becomes null.
- If the diameter passes through the root node, then the number of nodes in the path will be : Left subtree height + Right subtree height + 1
- However, if it does not pass through the root node, then the diameter will be MAXIMUM(left subtree diameter, right subtree diameter)
- The final diameter will be the maximum value of step 6 and step 7 , and this value will be returned.
- This process is continued in recursion till we encounter NULL nodes.

Time complexity : **O(N^2)** where there are N nodes in the Binary Tree.

The time complexity is $O(N^2)$ as for each node, we are calculating the height of the concerned tree separately and using the result to compute the diameter recursively.

Space Complexity: **O(log N)**, if a balanced tree, **O(N)** otherwise. Space complexity is due to recursion.

Pseudocode:

```
// Method to calculate the diameter
int diameter(Node root)
{
    // base case if tree is empty
    if (root == null)
        return 0;

    // get the height of left and right sub trees
    int lheight = height(root.left);
    int rheight = height(root.right);

    // get the diameter of left and right subtrees
    int ldiameter = diameter(root.left);
    int rdiameter = diameter(root.right);

    /* Return max of following three
    1) Diameter of left subtree
    2) Diameter of right subtree
    3) Height of left subtree + height of right subtree + 1
    */
    return MAXIMUM(lheight + rheight + 1,
                    MAXIMUM(ldiameter, rdiameter));
}
```

Approach 2: Using DFS in naïve way

1. We can run DFS N times .

2. First we can choose any node and find the farthest node from that node using depth first search .

3. We need to repeat the step 2 with all the nodes of the tree and store the maximum value .

4. This maximum value will then be the diameter of the tree.

Time Complexity

The above approach would work fine but time complexity for the above approach will be $O(N^2)$ as we run DFS for each node. This is quite high.

Better Approach

We can find the diameter of any tree using only 2 DFS run. **How ?**

Quick Explanation:

1. Take any arbitrary node as the root node .

2. Run DFS from that node and find the farthest node.

3. Let this node be x .

4. Now run DFS from this node to the farthest away node , let this node be y.

5. Now the count of all the nodes that come along the way of x and y (including them) is the diameter of the tree.

Why this works ?

61

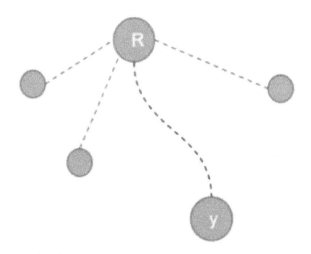

Whenever we run DFS we always reach one of the end points of diameter of the tree and from that node we are just finding the farthest node which turns out to be the diameter of the tree.

Let us proof this fact that on running DFS we always reach the end point of diameter of the tree

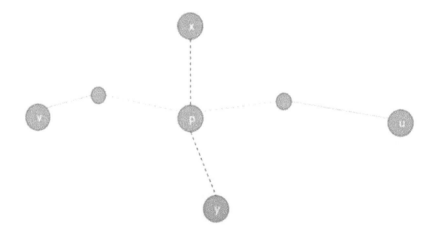

Proof by contradiction

We are considering x as the root of the tree

Assume that on running DFS first time from x and finding the farthest node we reach on node y .

Let us say y is not the end point of the diameter of the tree

and v-p-y is the actual diameter of the tree

In that case according to the above image we can write the equation

(note that if root of the tree lies on the diameter of the tree then distance xp is considered as 0)

xp + py < xp + pv

and

xp + py < xp + pu

On simplifying the above equations:

py < pv

and

py < pu

This cannot be true as y is at maximum distance from p and according to our assumption y is not on the diameter of the tree both statements cannot be true simultaneously .

So, our first assumption that node y does not lie on the diameter does not hold true and hence, after running the first DFS we reach node y which always lie on the diameter of the tree .

Example

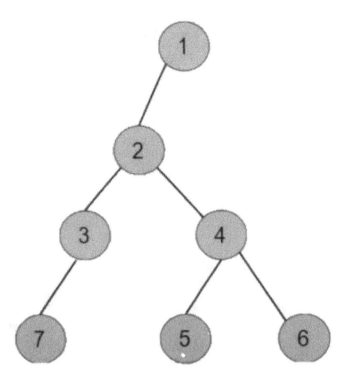

Suppose we want to find the diameter of the graph shown in the above image.

Let us take node 4 as our starting node (we can choose any node)

Now on running the depth first search for the first time, we will be able to find the one end of the diameter which will be 7 for this example.

Now on running DFS from 7 and finding the farthest node, we will reach 6 via path

7-3-2-4-6.

4. The count of nodes along the path is 5 which is the diameter of the tree in this example.

(Note - we could have also reached 6 via path 7-3-2-4-5 which would also have been the diameter of the tree as both count as farthest node with same value of distances)

5. In this way, we can find the diameter of any tree using only two DFS run .

Pseudocode:

```
// maxD represent the diameter of the tree
// maxNode represents node at maximum distance
int maxD = -1 , maxNode = -1 ;

// declaring the visited node as we will be using the DFS
int visited[N]

void createEdge( int a , int b , vector<int> graph[] ){

    // creating undireted edges between the connected nodes
    graph[a].push_back(b) ;
    graph[b].push_back(a) ;

}


void DFS( vector<int> graph[] , int node , int d )
{
    // marking the node as visited
    visited[node] = 1 ;

    // if the distance from root is greater then
    // maximum Distance then updating the maximum
    // value of distance also storing the maxNode
    // number as this node is now at the farthest distance
    if( d > maxD )
    {
        maxNode = node ;
        maxD = d ;
    }

    // applying the standard DFS
    for( auto x : graph[node] )
    {
        if( visited[x] == 0 )
        {
            DFS( graph , x , d+1 ) ;
```

```
            }
        }
    }

// Applyting DFS from node 1
    DFS( graph , 1 , 1 ) ;
    // we could have choosen any node in the graph
    // but for simplicity we have choosen node 1
    // making every node unvisited as we will be applying DFS
    maxD = -1 ;
    for( int i = 1 ; i<=8 ; i++ )
    {
        visited[i] = 0 ;
    }

    // applying the dfs for the second time as this
    // will give the diameter of the tree
    DFS( graph , maxNode , 1 ) ;


    // Maximum diameter of the tree
    ANSWER = maxD
```

Complexity Analysis

Time taken = 2 * N (N units of time is taken to run the depth first search once)

Hence, Time Complexity: **O(N)**.

There is no extra space required apart from some variables therefore the space required is constant.

Space Complexity: **O(1)**.

Insight:

Using this approach, we can find the two farthest points in a Binary Tree. Consider the situation where we represent games in a Tournament as a Binary Tree. Finding

66

the diameter in this case will give us two players who if face each other needs the maximum number of games to be conducted.

If the Binary Tree is balanced, there can be multiple diameters. Think on this carefully.

Check if a Binary Tree is Balanced by Height

A Binary tree is said to be balance if:

- The left subtree is balanced for each node.
- Right subtree is also balanced for each node.
- The absolute height difference of left and right subtree is not more than 1.

Further, all empty trees are always height balanced.

There are multiple interpretations of a Binary Tree being balanced and checking for one of these properties lead to checking if the Binary Tree is balanced:

- **Maximum path length of root to leaf node <= Minimum path length of root to leaf node**

As the Binary Tree is balanced, the maximum and minimum path length from root to a leaf node can be same if the Binary Tree is complete that is the last level "I" has 2^I leaf nodes.

If it is not complete but it is balanced, then a few leaf nodes are missing from the last level and the nodes in the previous level "I – 1" becomes a leaf node. These leaf nodes form the minimum path length. Hence, the maximum difference in path lengths will be 1.

- **Each level "I" has 2^I nodes except the last level where there can be less nodes**

The idea is same as the above point. If all levels are completely filled, then it is a complete Binary Tree and hence, it is balanced. If there are a few nodes missing in the last level, still then it is balanced as the maximum height difference is 1.

- **A complete Binary Tree is always Balanced**

This point should be clear from the explanation of the above two points.

- **All sub-trees of a Balanced Binary Tree are balanced**

This is because as the maximum height difference of the entire tree is 1, the sub-trees cannot have a height difference of greater than 1 as it would add up and make the entire tree unbalanced. Hence, all sub-trees have to be balanced.

68

We will take a straightforward and efficient approach. The key idea is to check if each sub-tree is balanced or not.

Algorithm:

Step 1: Start

Step 2: If the node is NULL then return 0.

Step 3: If left sub tree is not balanced then return -1.

Step 4: If the right sub tree is not balanced then return -1.

Step 5: If the absolute difference between height of left and right subtree is greater than 1,return -1 else return maximum out of left and right subtree's height + 1.

Step 6: End.

Example:

Considering the binary tree below:

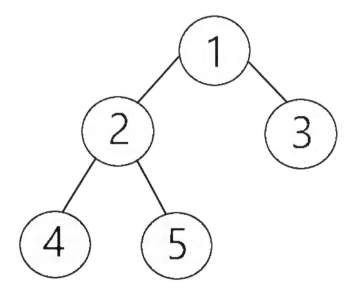

Firstly, our node is not NULL.

Hence, we proceed to check the height of left subtree first.

1. For the root node, the height of its left subtree is 2 (from node 1 to node 2 and node 2 to node 4). Similarly, the height of the right subtree is 1 (from node 1 to node 3). So, absolute difference in the height of left and right subtree is 1.

Hence, satisfying the condition that absolute difference of the height of left and right subtree is smaller than or equal to 1.

2. Similarly, for the node 2 the height of its left subtree is 1 (node 2 to node 4) and height of right subtree is also 1 (node 2 to node 5). Hence, the absolute difference of their heights is 0.

Hence, satisfying the condition that absolute difference of the height of left and right subtree is smaller than or equal to 1.

3. For node 4, node 5 and node 3 the absolute difference in their left and right subtrees is 0 since they do not have any children nodes.

Hence, satisfying the condition that absolute difference of the height of left and right subtree is smaller than or equal to 1.

This way all nodes satisfy the required condition. Hence, our binary tree is balanced.

Let us implement this via code :

```
// firstly, pass the root as argument to "balanced" function
int balanced(Node root)
{

    // if the root is NULL return 0
    if(root==NULL)
        return 0;
```

70

```
    //check if the left subtree's height is balanced. If no then
return -1
    int left_height = balanced(root ->left);
    if(left_height == -1)
        return -1;

    //check if the right subtree's height is balanced. If no then
return -1
    int right_height = balanced(root->right);
    if(right_height == -1)
        return -1;

    //if absolute difference of left subtree's height and right
subtree's height > 1 then return -1
    if(absolute(right_height - left_height)>1)
        return -1;

    // return maximum out of left subtree's height and right
subtree's height + 1
    return max(left_height, right_height) + 1;
}
```

The time complexity of this approach is O(N).

The space complexity is O(N) due to the stack where recursive calls are stored for all nodes till the leaf nodes are reached.

N is the number of nodes in the Binary Tree.

Insight:

This is an important concept as you will see that a Binary Tree reaches its full potential only when it is balanced by height.

There are techniques to ensure that our Binary Tree is balanced at all times and such trees are known as Self Balancing Binary Tree which will be explore later in this book.

Find number of Universal Value subtrees in Binary Tree

We need to find the number of sub-trees whose nodes have same value, called universal value subtree or simply univalue subtree.

What is universal value subtree?

Univalue tree : Tree having a same value for all the nodes and root too.

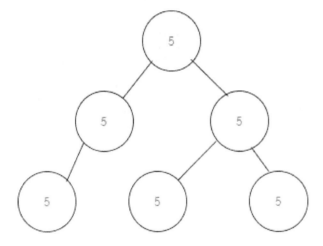

The binary tree given below is not universal. It has subtrees which have universal values. Leaves of a binary tree are always universal as they do not point to any node instead point to NULL.

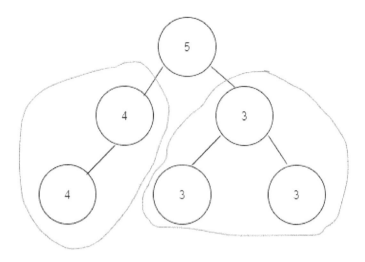

How many subtrees having universal values are present?

We count all the leaves due to the above-mentioned reason and then subtrees with same values and non-null nodes also.

In tree-Subtree containing same values i.e.

Number of such subtrees in the example = 2 ------> 1st equation

We will be counting the leaves that is total number of leaves = 3 -----> 2nd equation

Therefore, total number of universal subtrees = 1st equation + 2nd equation = 2+3 = 5

Now, we will go through the algorithm we will be implementing to find the number of universal value subtrees. We will be using bottom-up or postorder traversal to find number of univalued subtrees.

73

Brute Force approach

In a Binary Tree of N nodes, the number of subtrees is always N. This is because every node is a root of a sub-tree.

For a given sub-tree with M nodes, the worst case time complexity to check if it is a univalued tree is O(M).

On average, the number of nodes in a sub-tree is O(N). Hence, the steps of a Brute force approach will be:

- Get all sub-trees of a Binary Tree
- Check if the current sub-tree is univalued.

This approach will take $O(N^2)$ time complexity.

We can improve this with a simple observation:

- If a Binary Tree with root P is univalued, then the sub-trees rooted at the left and right child nodes are also univalued.

Explanation

When is the subtree considered to be univalue subtree?

- When the subtree's both left and right child nodes' values are equal to root's value.
- When they are leaves that is left and right nodes are null.
- When the left or right node is null, but the existing right or left node has value equal to the root's value.
- When the subtree does not satisfy these three conditions , then it is not a univalue subtree.

Efficient Algorithm

- Check if root is NULL. If true, then return 0 as no roots are present.
- Count Number of left and right subtrees by recursive calls.

- Check if right or left subtrees returned are univalued. If no, then return false.
- Check if left or right nodes exist .
- If right or left node's value is not equal to root's value, then return false and do not count.
- If any of the eliminating cases are not satisfied then it is a univalue subtree, so increment the count.
- Finally, after checking on every node return the count.

Pseudocode

```
bool countUniValueST(root , count)
{
    //basecase
    check if root==NULL:
        return true

    // all right & left subtrees through recursion and
    // store whether they're univalued or not
    bool left = countUniValueST(root->left, count)
    bool right =  countUniValueST(root->right , count)

    // all possible cases when the subtree is not univalued:
    if any of the left or right subtree is not univalued:
        return false
    if right node exists and right[DATA] NOT EQUAL TO root[DATA]:
        return false
    if left node exists and left[DATA] NOT EQUAL TO root[DATA]:
        return false

    // if any of the above conditions not satisfied:
    // increment subtree count
    count++
    return true
}
```

Explanation of step by step example:

```
input :        1
              / \
             3   3
            / \
           3   3
```

Now by counting we know that there are 4 univalued subtrees.

Since we are following bottom to up approach, we first traverse to the leaves. According to the conditions, they are counted as univalued. There are 3 leaves so univalued subtrees count is 3.

We will observe left part of the binary tree first.

```
    1  ----root
   /
  3  ---subroot
 /\
3  3 ---both leaves
```

After counting in the 2 leaves(3,3) , they are checked if they are not equal to subtree's root data .As both are equal to subroot's data so count is incremented.

```
1  ---root
 \
   3  ---leaf
```

3 being leaf is counted as univalued but it is not equal to the root's value ,so its returned false. Now, as we have reached the root, we return the count of univalued subtrees which is 4.

Time Complexity:

This code follows a linear time complexity O(N), where N means the number of nodes of the tree.

Space Complexity:

Auxiliary space used is O(h) for the recursion call stack , where h is the height of the binary tree as we are recursively travelling till h height.

Hence, finding the number of univalued subtrees is same as a single traversal from an algorithmic point of view. Compare this with the brute force approach. We improved the time complexity from $O(N^2)$ to O(N).

Insight:

This may seem to be just a practice problem, but this has some key applications in real problems. For example, in specific systems, we want to compress the Binary Tree to reduce duplicates and such univalued sub-trees can be compressed to a single node.

Can you think of such a situation?

Counting subtrees where nodes sum to a specific value

We will learn about counting the subtrees in a Binary Tree whose nodes sum to a given value. We will be trying different methods to solve our problem in depth. We will solve it in O(N) time complexity and O(H) space complexity where N is number of nodes and H is the height of the tree.

Problem:

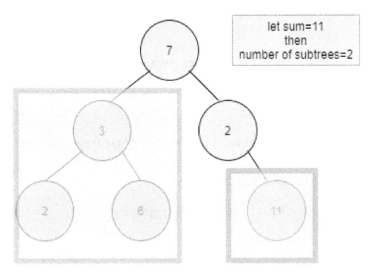

Let us say we need to find count of subtrees whose nodes sum to 11. In the example subtree, the whole left subtree's nodes sum up to 11 and the leaf itself is 11.So the total number of subtrees whose nodes added up to 11 were 2.

Brute Force approach:

The first approach that comes to mind when we see this question is to go to the root and check if the sum of root + leftnode + rightnode is equal to sum, else move to the next right or left node and repeat the same. Also check if entire tree's sum is equal to the given value.

This approach will have the time complexity of **O(N²)** as you check for each and every node.

So, let us examine few methods through which we can count subtrees whose sum would be equal to say, x.

1.BFS method:

In BFS or level wise traversal , the idea is to go through each node in level wise fashion and find the subtrees of each node whose sum equals the given value and count all such subtrees.

Algorithm:

- X=Sum to search for.
- SUM=Subtree Sum(left+right+root).
- Traverse each node by level order traversal.
- Calculate sum of all nodes that is from node till the null node
- Check if SUM=X
- If yes,Increment the count.
- Repeat for all other nodes traversed level wise.

Pseudocode:

```
INT subtreeSum(ROOT)
{
   CHECK:( ROOT=NULL)
        RETURN 0
   RETURN ROOT[VALUE]+subtreeSum(ROOT->LEFT)+subtreeSum(ROOT-
>RIGHT)
}

INT checkSubtreeSumX(ROOT,LEVEL,X,REFERENCE(count))
{
    CHECK(ROOT==NULL): RETURN 0
    CHECK: (LEVEL=1 && subtreeSum(ROOT)=X)
    count++;

    if(LEVEL>1)
```

```
    {
        checkSubtreeSumX(ROOT->RIGHT,LEVEL-1,X,count);
        checkSubtreeSumX(ROOT->RIGHT,LEVEL-1,X,count);
    }

    return ROOT[VALUE];
}
INT countSubtreescheckroot(ROOT,X)
{   count=0;
    h = HEIGHT(ROOT)
    int i;
  LOOP(i:1 to h )
     checkSubtreeSumX(ROOT, i,X,count);\
    RETURN count
}
```

Step by step explanation

Level 1

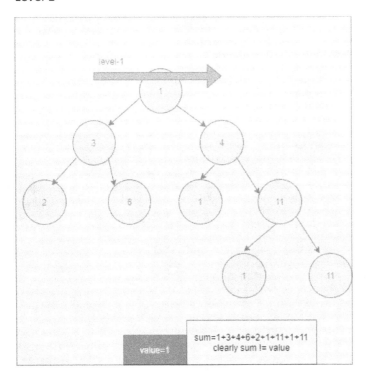

Therefore count=0 now.

LEVEL-2, Left node

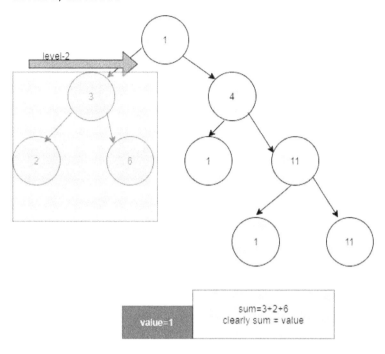

sum=3+2+6
clearly sum = value

value=1

The count=0 as sum=11 and sum!=value.

Right Node

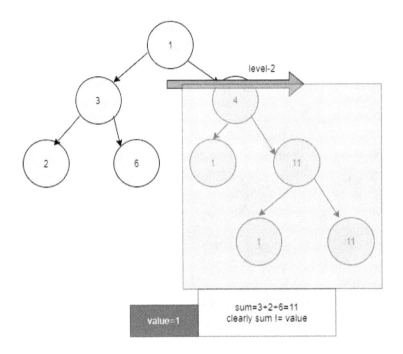

sum=3+2+6=11
clearly sum != value

value=1

Similarly, it will happen for all the values whose nodes' sum is not equal to 1.

LEVEL-3

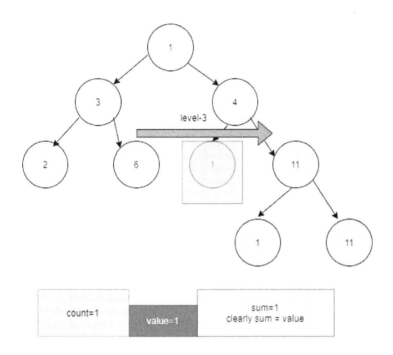

As the leaf[value]=1 therefore it being equal to value , the count=1

count=1, LEVEL-4

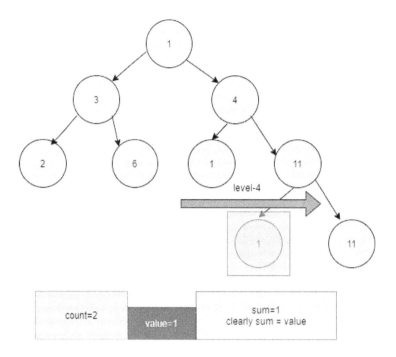

Now , count=2. So later no subtrees or leaves are left , so it returns the count as 2.

Time and space complexity:

Time Complexity - **O(N²)**

As the recursive call is being called for N-i times inside for loop which runs for n times , the time complexity is **O(N²)** where N is number of nodes.

Space Complexity - **O(h)** where h is the height of the tree.

BFS method is better than brute force but not the best one to use considering its time complexity. We can do better by using DFS methods.

2. Iterative method:

We will be now using post order traversal iteratively, to find the subtrees having the total nodes sum equal to the value specified.

We will be using two stacks to traverse in postorder and then use the stack having elements in postorder fashion to find the count of the subtrees whose sum of all its nodes is equal to the given value, X.

Algorithm:

- X=Specified value
- count=Subtrees count
- Store all nodes in a stack in postorder fashion.
- Select the top and check if its left and right nodes exists.
- If yes then check if the node's value is equal to X.
- If the value=X then increment the count.
- If No then:
- Store the left, right nodes in a stack by calling postorder function and derive the sum by adding all the top elements and popping them up. Check if their sum=X. If yes, then increment the count.
- Pop the top and continue same steps with the next node until the stack is empty.

Pseudocode

```
// stack of node* datatype.
(node*)stack postorder(ROOT)
{
    two stacks : s1,s2
    UNTIL s1 is EMPTY:
        ROOT=s1.top
        s1.pop
        if ROOT->LEFT NOT NULL:
            s1.PUSH(ROOT->LEFT)
        if ROOT->RIGHT NOT NULL:
            s1.PUSH(ROOT->RIGHT)
        s2.PUSH(ROOT)
    RETURN s2
}

INT countSubtreesum(ROOT,X,stack<node*> s)
{
```

```
UNTIL s is EMPTY:
  if s.top->left and s.top->right are NULL
    check s.top(value)=x
  if yes:count++;
  else
  store values of each node postorderly in subs.
  UNTIL subs is EMPTY:
    Add all the elements to sum
    if sum=X: count++
}
RETURN count
```

Step by step output

We will see how postorder traversal is being done iteratively using two stacks:

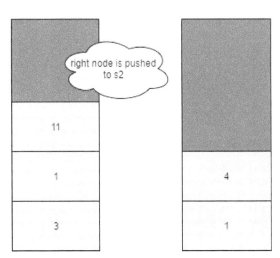

Similar arrangements happen until the s1 is empty.

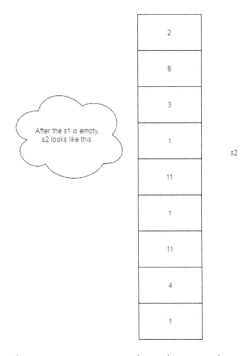

The process to count the subtrees whose sum=x here x=1:

So, whenever the node present in the stack points to NULL and has no right and left children that is if they are leaves, we just need to check if its value is equal to 1.

If yes, then we increment the count.

What if the node is not NULL and points to left or right or both?

We store all the nodes of that node in a stack in a postorder way. Later we will be adding all the nodes values to the sum and checking if its equal to 1.

The tree is:

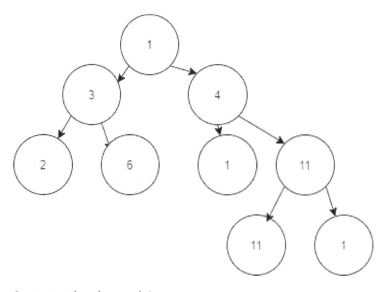

So currently , the stack is :

2 6 3 1 11 1 11 4 1

We will take 2,store it in root and pop it, and we can see that it is a leaf and as 2!=1 ,

we will take 6, as 6!=1, same goes for it.

But 3 is not leaf so we will call postorder function and store 2,6 and 3 in subs stack.

We will add them ,

```
sum=2
pop(2)
```

```
sum=2+6
pop(6)
sum=8+3=11
pop(3)
```

As stack is empty, we come out of loop

sum=11 and sum!=1

So, no increment of count. This will continue till stack is empty and later the count is returned.

As there are two 1s which are leafs ,so count=2.

Time and Space Complexity:

Due to stacks being used it occupies extra space and worst time complexity is O(n^2).We can counter these problems using recursive approach.

3. Recursive method:

Algorithm

We will be now using post order traversal recursively, to find the subtrees having the total nodes sum equal to the value specified.

- If ROOT:=NULL then return 0
- Traverse through the left subtre.
- Traverse through the right subtree.
- Check for LEFT[VALUE]+RIGHT[VALUE]+ROOT[VALUE]:=target sum.
- If yes then increment the count.
- Then return the sum of subtrees.
- Check whether the main root and the left and right subtree sum is equal to target sum.
- If yes then increment count.
- Return the count of subtrees with sum equal to target sum.

90

Pseudocode

```
INT helper(ROOT,TSUM,(REFERENCE)COUNT)
{
    CHECK:( ROOT=NULL)
      RETURN 0
    LEFTSUBTREE :=helper(ROOT->LEFT,TSUM,COUNT)
    RIGHTSUBTREE :=helper(ROOT->RIGHT,TSUM,COUNT)
    CHECK TSUM=LEFTSUBTREE+RIGHTSUBTREE+ROOT[VALUE]
    IF YES: COUNT:=COUNT+1
      RETURN SUM
}
INT countSubtrees(ROOT,TSUM)
{
 COUNT:=0
 CHECK:( ROOT=NULL)
 RETURN 0
 LEFTSUBTREE :=helper(ROOT->LEFT,TSUM,COUNT)
 RIGHTSUBTREE :=helper(ROOT->RIGHT,TSUM,COUNT)
 CHECK TSUM=LEFTSUBTREE+RIGHTSUBTREE+ROOT[VALUE]
 IF YES: COUNT:=COUNT+1
   RETURN COUNT
}
```

Time and Space Complexity

Time complexity of this code is O(N) where N is the number of nodes of the binary tree and the space complexity of the problem is O(h) where h is the height of the binary tree.

Now you know how to count number of subtrees which sum up to a specific value in depth.

Insight:

If you think carefully, this is similar to our previous problem (univalued subtrees) and sum of nodes can be another property that can be compressed to a single node.

91

Can you think of properties of a sub-tree that can be a significant factor for compression?

Find if a given Binary Tree is a Sub-Tree of another Binary Tree

A sub-tree is a tree that is the subset of a bigger binary tree. We will find out different ways to find out if a given binary tree is a sub-tree of another binary tree. To understand this concept better, let us consider an example of a tree 'Target':

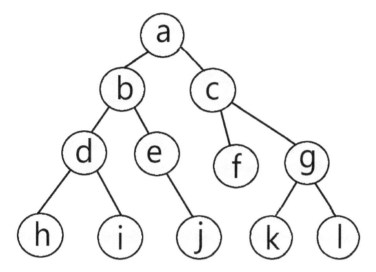

Now, let us consider another tree called 'Source'.

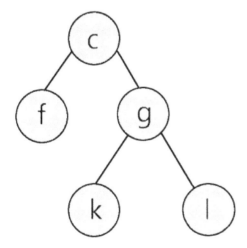

We will start to check from the root node of 'Target', that is 'a'. Since, 'a' is not present in 'Source' tree, then we move on to the next node in the left subtree.

Upon further iterations, we will get to know that none of the nodes of the 'Source' tree exist in left-subtree of 'Target' tree. Then, we move on to the right subtree of 'Target' tree. Here, the node 'c' of 'Target' matches the first node of 'Source' tree. Then, we explore the left subtree of the node 'c' of target. Node 'f' also matches the node in 'source' tree. In similar fashion, we iterate and get to know that the entire right-subtree of 'Target' tree matches the 'Source' tree.

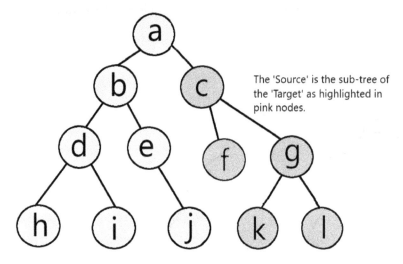

The 'Source' is the sub-tree of the 'Target' as highlighted in pink nodes.

Therefore, 'Source' is the sub-tree of the 'Target' tree.

Hence, in this way we can find out if a tree is the sub-tree of another binary tree. However, if 'Source' would have been as below, then it would not have been a sub-tree of 'Target' due to the presence of extra 'h' node in the left-subtree of 'f' node.

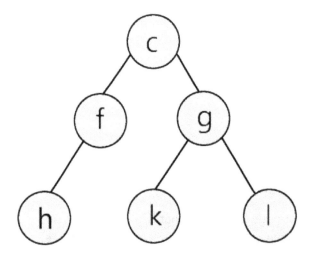

94

There are different approaches that can be followed to solve this problem. We will take two approaches:

- Brute force (using recursion)
- Efficient approach (using pre-order and in-order traversal)

Approach 1: Recursion

In this approach, for every node at the "target" tree, we check if the nodes of the "source" tree are present in the same structure. Hence, for every possible sub-tree in target tree, we match every node of source tree.

Let us assume that there are N nodes in "target" tree and M nodes in "source" tree.

Algorithm:

Within the function "subtree",

Step 1: If the 'Source' tree is null then return 1

Step 2: If the 'Target' tree is null then return 0

Step 3: If 'Target' and 'Source' are identical, then return 1

Step 4: Call function "subtree" by passing arguments- left node of the 'target' tree and the root node of 'source' tree and call function "subtree" by passing arguments - right node of 'target' tree and root node of 'source' tree.

If any of them executes to true, return true.

Explanation:

In the above algorithm, we start by creating a function "subtree". In this function, we provide first base condition to return 1 if the 'Source' tree is null. Since, any null tree is a sub-tree of all trees.

Then, we give another base condition if a 'Target' tree is null then no tree can be its sub-tree. Hence, we return 0.

95

Then, we define third base condition. If the 'Target' tree and 'Source' tree are identical then, we return 1. We check this condition by calling function "identical". This function we check if nodes passed as arguments are both null then return 1.

Else if both are not null then, return true if all of the below 3 conditions are true:

Data of node of "Target" and "Source" tree are equal.

Data of left node of "Target" and "Source" tree are equal (via recursion)

Data of right node of "Target" and "Source" tree are equal (via recursion)

Else, we return false if one node is null and one isn't.

Considering the below mentioned trees. Tree 'Source':

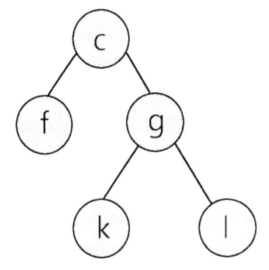

Tree 'Target':

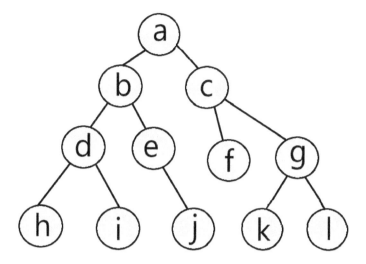

In the function "subtree", neither 'Source' nor 'Target' null. Hence, we check third condition if the two trees are identical. We call function "identical".

Now, we do not enter in its condition 1 since both are not NULL. Following the condition two, we check if 'Source' and 'Target' nodes are equal. Now this condition is not true for the root node of 'Target' and 'Source' hence we return false. Now the control comes back to "subtree" function.

Now, we come to the last condition of subtree and recursively call the subtree function again by passing left node and right node of 'Target' respectively along with root node of 'Source'.

This way upon, recursion we will return true when the right subtree of the 'Target' is executed, since it exactly matches 'Source'.

Let us have a look at the code:

```
// identical function which we will call in "subtree" function
// Compares all nodes one by one

int identical(struct node* a, struct node* b)
{
  //if both nodes are null then return true
  if (a==NULL && b==NULL)
    return(true);
```

```
   // if both are not null then return true if all
   // three mentioned conditions are true
   else if (a!=NULL && b!=NULL)
   {
     return( (a->data == b->data) &&
             (identical(a->left, b->left)) &&
             (identical(a->right, b->right)));
   }

   //if one node is null and one is not null then return false
   else return(false);
}
```

Now, let us define the function "subtree":

```
int subtree(node* a, node* b)
{
   //if source tree is null then return 1
   if(b == NULL){return 1;}

   //if target tree is null then return 0
   if(a == NULL){return 0;}

   // We call identical function here and if a
   // and b are identical then return 1

   if(identical(a,b)){
      return 1;
   }

   /* Recursively call subtree function with arguments :
   left node of 'Target' and root node of 'Source' AND
   right node of 'Target' and root node of 'Source'.
   If any of them returns true then the answer returned is true
   */

   return(subtree(a->left,b)|| subtree(a->right,b));
}
```

The Time complexity will be O(N x M).

The space complexity will be O(N) since the 'N' refers to the number of nodes here.

Approach 2: Pre-Order and In-order Traversal Method

A binary tree can be constructed if 2 different traversals are given. If any one of the traversal methods is In-order then, we can construct the binary tree from given combination of traversals {like in-order + pre-order}.

To accomplish our task of finding if a tree is a sub-tree of another tree or not, we arrange both 'Target' and 'Source' in preorder and inorder traversals. If the inorder and preorder traversals of 'Source' is substring of inorder and preorder traversal of 'Target' respectively then the 'Source' is said to be the sub-tree of 'Target'.

The Algorithm is :

- Step 1: Find out the preorder and inorder traversals of 'Target' and save them in arrays.
- Step 2: Find out the preorder and inorder traversals of 'Source' and save them in arrays.
- Step 3: Check if inorder traversal of 'Source' is a sub-array of inorder traversal of 'Target'
- Step 4: Check if preorder traversal of 'Source' is a sub-array of preorder traversal of 'Target'
- Step 5: If step 3 and 4 holds true, then 'Source' is a sub-tree of 'Target'.

Consider the 'Target' as below:

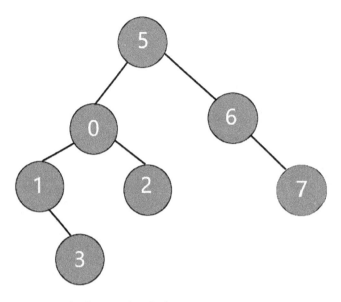

Consider the 'Source' as below:

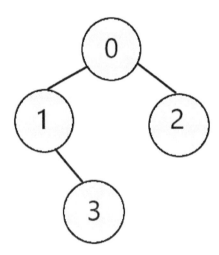

The Inorder Traversal of 'Target' is : {1,3,0,2,5,6,7}

The Inroder Traversal of 'Source' is : {1,3,0,2}

The Preorder Traversal of 'Target' is : {5,0,1,3,2,6,7}

The Preorder Traversal of 'Source' is : {0,1,3,2}

Clearly, the arrays of 'Source' are substrings of arrays of 'Target'. Hence, it is a sub-tree.

100

Let us see the pseudocode:

Firstly, we define the function to determine the Inorder Traversal.

```
/* In this function, we pass the root node of the tree,
   character array and i via reference as it represents
   the index of array
*/
void Inorder(Node* root, char arr[], int& i)
{

    /*If the root is NULL, then we put empty char
    in array location
    and return */

    if (root == NULL)
    {
        arr[i++] = ' ';
        return;
    }
    /*Else, we recursively call the Inorder Function
    till all nodes on the left-subtree are traversed*/
    Inorder(root->left, arr, i);

    // Then, we traverse the root node
    arr[i++] = root->key;

    // Finally, we traverse the right sub-tree
    Inorder(root->right, arr, i);
}
```

Then, we define the Pre-order Traversal :

```
/* In the similar fashion as above, we pass the root node,
   character array and index of array by reference as arguments
*/
void Preorder(Node* root, char arr[], int& i)
{
    // If the root is NULL then we pass empty character
```

101

```
    // to the array Then, we return
    if (root == NULL)
    {
        arr[i++] = ' ';
        return;
    }
    // Firstly, we traverse the root node
    arr[i++] = root->key;

    // Then, we traverse the left sub-tree Recursively
    Preorder(root->left, arr, i);

    // Finally, we recursivelly traverse the right sub-tree
    Preorder(root->right, arr, i);
}
```

Following is the main function that uses in-order and pre-order traversals:

```
bool isSubtree(Node Target, Node Source)
{
    /* Firstly, define the base case :
    - If Source is NULL then return True
    - If Target is NULL then return False
    */

    if (Source == NULL)
        return true;
    if (Target == NULL)
        return false;

    /*Now, initialize the variables m and n by 0
     as they represent the array indexes of 'Target'
     and 'Source' Traversal arrays
    */
    int i = 0, j = 0;

    //declare the arrays
    char inTarget[100], inSource[100];

    //Now, call the function Inorder for target and source trees
    Inorder(Target, inTarget, i);
    Inorder(Source, inSource, j);
```

```
        inTarget[i] = '\0', inSource[j] = '\0';

        // If inSource[] is not a substring of inTarget[]
        // then return false
        if (strstr(inTarget, inSource) == NULL)
            return false;

        i = 0, j = 0;
        char preTarget[100], preSource[100];

        // Calling Preorder Function to store the preorder traversals

        Preorder(Target, preTarget, i);
        Preorder(Source, preSource, j);

        preTarget[i] = '\0', preSource[j] = '\0';

        /* If preSource[] is not a substring of preTarget[],
           return false
           Else return true*/
        return (strstr(preTarget, preSource) != NULL);
}
```

This method takes time complexity of O(N) and Space complexity of O(N).

Note:

If you analyze carefully, in our second approach, we reduced the Binary Tree to a list of numbers and reduced the problem to check if a list exists within another list. This is important as it brings in two key ideas:

- Restructure the problem to solve it efficiently
- A Binary Tree can be seen as a list or just a single number (hash of the list).

This idea can help you solve several challenging problems.

Insight:

Checking if two data points or Data Structures are similar is a key operation in any field for example, finding similarity between two DNA to find if two animals can from the same source or crossed each other at some point.

Similarly, the way you use Binary Tree determines the use of this approach.

Check if a Binary Tree has duplicate values

Given a Binary Tree, we will develop an algorithm to check if it has duplicate values. This can be done in linear time O(N) where there are N elements in the Binary Tree.

In case of Linear data structures like an array or Linked List, we can simply traverse them in one way and check if two values are same. Trees are nonlinear data structures and therefore, it has multiple ways of traversal as we discussed previously (like inorder).

A simple way to find out if the tree has two nodes that have same data value is to traverse the tree and store the value in an Array and then checking if the Array has any entries that have the same value.

To traverse the tree, we can use any of the following:

- Inorder traversal
- Preorder traversal
- Postorder traversal

For illustration, we will be using Preorder traversal, a traversal in which root is visited first then the left subtree and later the right subtree. While traversing, we store the value of the nodes in an Array and then, it can be check if Array contains any duplicate elements.

Note: We are using Array List since the number of nodes in the tree are unknown (we do not require to specify size for an Array List during its initialization), an array can also be used if number of nodes is known beforehand or we can traverse the tree once to find out total number of nodes so that we are able to specify size of array that will store the data values.

Steps:

- Do preorder traversal of Binary Tree
- For every node:
  - Check if it exists in our array. If it does, tree has duplicate values.
  - Insert value of current node in array

Pseudocode:

```
traversal(root,arr);

boolean flag=false;
for(int i=0;i<arr.size();i++)
{
        for(int j=i+1;j<arr.size();j++)
        {
                if(arr.get(i)==arr.get(j))
                {
                        flag=true;
                        break;
                }
        }
}
```

Time Complexity: **O(N²)**

O(N²) is required to check for duplicates in the ArrayList as there are nested for loop. It takes a total of O(N²) time and O(N) is required for tree traversal as there are a total of N nodes to be traversed. O(N²) is the dominant term, thus O(N²) + O(N) = O(N²)

Space Complexity: **O(N)**

(Size of Array List is n as it stores the total number of nodes in tree)

We can reduce the time for finding duplicates to O(n) by using Hash Map but even then, we are traversing the Array List at least once.

A better way is to use a Hash Map and avoid use of Array List all together and traverse the tree only once. This way the problem can be solved in O(N) time.

Approach:

- We traverse the given tree
- For every node:
    - we check if it's data value already exists in the Hash Map.
    - If it does not exist, then we put it into the Hash Map.

106

o   If it exists already that is there is a duplicate and we return true. To
   check if an element exists in Hash Map already, it only takes O(1) time.

```
        6
      /   \
    10      9
   /  \    / \
 12    6  5   4
```

For example, in the given tree above, we traverse using preorder traversal.

So, when we start, we check if root that is 6 is present in HashMap already. As it is
not, we put it in the HashMap. Next, we go to 10 according to preorder and check if
it is present, if not we put in the HashMap, and so on. When we come to the 6
which is the right child of 10 ,we check if it is present in the map already and we
find that it is, as we already have put 6 in the map because 6 was the root element
and therefore, we have found a duplicate and we return true. Suppose you have a
tree which has no duplicates then we keep putting elements in the map and finally
when we have traversed the whole tree, false is returned.

Pseudocode:

```java
boolean traversal(Node root, HashMap<Integer, Integer> map)
{
        if(root==null)
        {
                return false;
        }
        if(map.containsKey(root.data))
        {
                //map contains the element already
                // that is there is a duplicate
                return true;
        }

        // as root is not null and not already in map,add
        // its data value to map
        map.put(root.data,0);

        //checking if duplicate is present in left
```

107

```
        // OR right subtree
        return traversal(root.left,map) ||
                traversal(root.right,map);

}
```

Time Complexity: **O(N)**

In worst case, we will be traversing the whole tree and algorithm would take O(N) time as tree has n nodes.

Space Complexity: **O(N)**

In worst case that is when no duplicates are present, we will be storing all the nodes data value in the Map and would require O(N) space as tree has a total of n nodes.

Insight:

This is simple problem but involve some key ideas that can help formulate efficient solutions to challenging problems. An extension of the problem is to find if there are duplicate sub-trees in a Binary Tree. This can be solved using the insights from the previous two problems we explored.

Think deeply about this extended problem.

Find nodes which are at a distance k from root in a Binary Tree

We are given the root of a tree, and an integer K. We need to print all the nodes which are at a distance K from the root. Distance is the number of edges in the path from the source node (Root node in our case) to the destination node.

For example, if the given tree is:

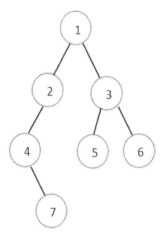

Here, the root is 1. If k is 2, then the output should be 4, 5 and 6 as they are at a distance of 2 from the root.

This problem can be solved using a general traversal technique like:

- Breadth First Search
- Depth First Search
- Level Order Traversal

In Depth First Search (DFS) and Breadth First Search (BFS), we can keep track of the level of each node by adding 1 to each level of traversal. When the level is K, the current node is at a distance of K from the root node.

In Level Order traversal, we shall get all nodes at level K.

109

This problem can be easily solved using general recursion:

- We will make a recursion function say printNodes(node root, int k) .
- This function will recursively call itself in its left and right children, with a distance of k-1.
- Finally, when k=0 is encountered, we will print the value in the current node. This node will be at a distance of k from the root.

Walkthrough

Let us walk through the procedure with our given example.

Initially, the root of the tree is 1 and k = 2. Since k is not equal to 0, we will recursively call the tree with its left child as the root and k-1. Hence, the function printNodes(root->left, 1) will be called.

Our new root will then be 2 and k =1. Again, k is not 0, hence we will call the function printNodes(root->left, 0).

Now, our root is 4 and this time, k=0. So, we will print the data in the given root, as this node will be at a distance of k=2 from the original root.

Similarly, the recursive function will be called in the right subtrees until we get a NULL value, or until k=0.

The following graph depicts the recursion route. (The function name printNodes is abbreviated to pN)

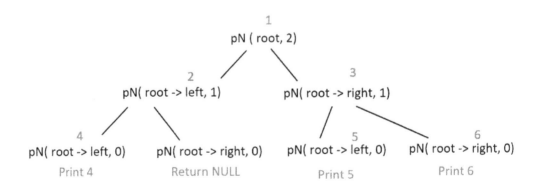

Pseudocode:

```
void printNodes(node root , int k)
{
    if(root == NULL)
        return;

    if( k == 0 )
    {
        print( root->data );
        return ;
    }
    else
    {
        printNodes( root->left, k - 1 ) ;
        printNodes( root->right, k - 1 ) ;
    }
}
```

Time complexity: O(N)

Space complexity: O(N) , where N is the number of nodes.

Insight: This is a pretty easy problem compared to the problems we have already explored. The challenge comes in a modification in the problem statement where we need to find all nodes at a distance K from any given node (can be other than the root node).

This is the problem we will explore next but before moving on, spend some time to analyze if you can solve this problem efficiently using the ideas we have explored.

111

Finding nodes at distance K from a given node

As an extension to our previous problem, we will explore approaches to find out the nodes at distance K from the given node.

Let us assume we have a binary tree. Let the node given to us be 'Target Node'. Now, we need to find all nodes at distance k from 'Target Node'. Those k nodes could be parent as well as child nodes of the 'Target Node'.

We can follow two major techniques:

1. Breadth First Traversal:

In this method, we perform the Breadth First Search and recursively print the k left child nodes of 'Target Node'. Then in similar fashion print the k right nodes of 'Target Node'. Afterwards, we can traverse the parent node.

2. Percolate Distance:

In this method, we perform the Depth First Search and then at each node, we calculate the distance from the 'Target Node'.

Breadth First Traversal:

1.For the first approach of Breadth First Search we have to convert the binary tree to an Undirected graph. The graph can be made by post-order traversal. We can make adjacency list or adjacent matrix.

2. Now, using Breadth First Search, we will find the k nodes around our 'Target Node'. We will keep storing them in array.

3. We return the array containing all nodes.

Complexity Analysis:

The space complexity will be **O(N)** as we go to each node twice when we make graph.

The time complexity will be **O(N)** as Binary Tree is always a sparse graph (think why?)

Pseudocode:

```
//function to calculate distance of nodes from target

vector<int> distanceK(Tree* root, Tree* target, int K) {
    if(root == nullptr || target == nullptr || K < 0){
        return {};
    }

    if(K == 0){
        return {target->val};
    }

    // call function Graph to make graph
    unordered_map<int, vector<int>> graph;
    Graph(root, graph);

    // BFS to find target node
    unordered_set<int> visited;

    queue<pair<int, int>> q;
    q.emplace(make_pair(target->val, 0));

    //vector to store nodes
    vector<int> result;

    while(!q.empty()){
        pair<int, int> curr = q.front();
        q.pop();
        visited.insert(curr.first);

        for(auto &neighbor : graph[curr.first]){
            if(visited.count(neighbor) == 0){
                int distance = curr.second + 1;
                if(distance == K){
                    result.emplace_back(neighbor);
```

```
            }
            else if(distance < K){
                q.emplace(make_pair(neighbor, distance));
            }
          }
        }
      }
    }

    return result;
}
```

Step by step explanation:

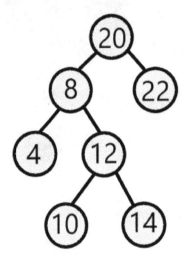

For above tree, firstly we check if the root or target is NULL or if the distance k is less than 0. If so, then we return.

If k is equivalent to 0 then we return the value of the node since it means that we have reached the target node back.

Then, we build a graph by traversing through its left and right subtree and inserting values recursively.

For Breadth First Search, we first create unordered set named "visited" to keep a track of all visited nodes and a queue named "q". The queue will keep pairs of nodes along with its corresponding distance from target.

Then we make vector "result". It will store the final result.

114

Now, we enter a while loop that traverses until the queue "q" is empty. This means it will keep iterating until all neighboring nodes of target have been visited.

Within While Loop:

- We make a pair "curr", It represents the current pair of nodes and its distance. We store this value from the top value of queue "q" and then pop that value from "q".
- Then, this value is stored in visited vector to keep a record of visited nodes.
- Then, we enter another for loop:
- Then we check if the visited count is 0. If so, we declare variable "distance" and initialize it with second value of "curr" (that is the distance) + 1.
- Now, if the distance becomes equivalent to "k" then we will insert this node to result vector. Else if the distance is less than k, then we must keep iterating. Hence, we insert pair of neighbors and its distance to queue "q".
- In the end after the queue is empty, we get out of our while loop and return result. It will contain all neighboring k nodes of our tree.

The time complexity of this approach is O(N) which is optimal, but the issue is that we need to convert the Binary Tree to an undirected graph which is an overhead.

Percolate Distance:

In this method, we traverse the tree and check if the current node is the 'Target Node'. When we get them, we perform the pre-order traversal to find all neighboring nodes at k distance.

In this method, the striking difference is that we consider the target node as the root node.

Consider an example, suppose we have a root node from which our target node is at distance 3, in right branch. Then, any node at distance k-3 in left branch will be returned.

Complexity Analysis:

- The space complexity will be O(N)
- The time complexity will be O(N)

Implementation:

There are 4 key steps that we take care of :

- If the root==target then return all nodes in the subtree at distance k.
- If the target lies in left subtree of node at distance 'm', then we will find the nodes at distance k-m in right branch.
- In similar fashion we move forward with right branch of node.
- If we cannot find target in either branch of the tree, then we will stop.

Pseudocode:

```
void percolate(root, k)
{
        if(root==NULL || k<0)
                return ;

        if(k==0)
        {
                print( root->data );
                return;
        }

        percolate(root->left, k-1);
        percolate(root->right, k-1);

}

int print(root, target, k)
{
        if(root==NULL)
                return -1;
        if(root==target)
        {
                percolate(root,k);
                return 1;
        }
        int left = print(root->left,target,k);
        int right = print(root->right,target,k);

        if(left!=-1)
        {
```

```
            if(left==k)
            {
                print( root->data );
            }
        percolate(root->right,k-left-1);
            return left+1;
        }

        if(right!=-1)
        {
                if(right==k){
                        print( root->data );
        }

                percolate(root->left,k-right-1);
                return right+1;
        }
        return -1;
}
```

Step by step explanation:

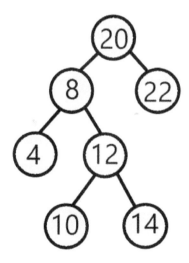

We can follow the below approach to traverse our above tree taken as example and find the k nearest neighbors. Percolate function is a recursive function that traverses left and right sub-tree of our given tree.

Firstly, let us understand the percolate function. If the root is null or k is smaller than 0, we return.

If k is 0 then we return the value of node and return.

In the print function, we have root of tree, target and distance k as arguments. If the root is null, we return -1.

If the root is equivalent to the target, we call percolate function with root and k as arguments.

Then, we declare "left" integer variable and store the value returned by function print in it recursively. This is to check if there is any null node. If there is a null node then value of -1 will be returned to "left".

Similar to "left", we have "right". We follow same procedure for the right subtree too.

Now, if the left is not equal to -1, that is it does not encounter null node, then we check the following:

If the left is equivalent to "k" then we print the value of left i.e root->data.

Since this means that the node is located at distance.

Then we call percolate function again, with distance "k-left-1", because we are going to node that is one step away from the current node. Hence, at left-1 distance. And since we have to traverse k nodes hence k-left-1.

In similar fashion, we check value for "right" integer variable and traverse the nodes. In the end we would have printed all the nodes at k distance in our tree.

Time Complexity: O(N)

Space Complexity: O(N) because of stack size.

Insight:

In terms of performance and space, both algorithms are equivalent, but the second approach is important as we are able to avoid modifying the input data (that is the Binary Tree).

118

In real systems, it is important that the input data is not modified even if there is no such requirements. When needed, a copy of the input is used.

Find ancestors of a given node in a binary tree

Given a binary tree, we need to find the ancestors of a particular node. An ancestor is a node that is present in the upper layer of a given node. Since the problem revolves around binary trees, a particular node can have at most 2 children so the ancestor of any given node will be its parent node and the ancestor of the parent node will be its parent node (grandparent node for the particular node in question). We will be printing the ancestors of a particular node until we reach the root of the binary tree.

Let us understand this using a figure.

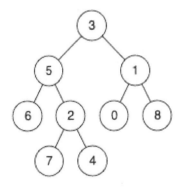

- Ancestors of node 3: None (since the root node)
- Ancestors of node 5: 3
- Ancestors of node 1: 3
- Ancestors of node 6: 5, 3
- Ancestors of node 2: 5, 3
- Ancestors of node 0: 1, 3
- Ancestors of node 8: 1, 3
- Ancestors of node 7: 2, 5, 3
- Ancestors of node 4: 2, 5, 3

We will solve this using both:

- Recursive solution

- Iterative solution

Idea behind solving this problem

1. Recursive solution

To solve this problem using recursion, first traverse the binary tree in a postorder fashion. A postorder traversal is one where the left subtree is traversed first, followed by the right subtree and the root is traversed at the end. If the given node is found at either the left subtree or the right subtree for any node, then the current node in the traversal would be the ancestor of the node.

The algorithm for this approach is as follows:

- Input the binary tree and the key_node whose ancestors are to be printed.
- Traverse all the nodes of the tree and perform recursive post order traversal.
- Until the key_node is found, traverse the left and right sub trees recursively.
- Once the key_node is reached, return the data of the nodes in the path.

2. Iterative solution

To solve this problem using recursion, we need to store the parent node of all the nodes in the tree explicitly (using a map in C++ or a dictionary in Python). Then we would traverse the binary tree in an iterative preorder fashion.

An iterative preorder traversal is similar to the regular preorder traversal: start at the root node and traverse the left subtree followed by traversing the right subtree. Set the parent pointer of each node and print the ancestors of the given node using the explicit map that is used to store all the nodes in the binary tree.

The algorithm for this approach is as follows:

- Input the binary tree and the key_node whose ancestors are to be printed.
- Traverse all the nodes of the tree and perform iterative post order traversal.
- Stop the traversal when the desired key_node is reached.
- Store the ancestors of the nodes while traversing in a stack.

121

- Once we reach the key_node, print the stack.

Pseudocode for recursive approach

```
// Recursive function to print all ancestors of a given
// node in a binary tree.
// The function returns true if the node is found in the
// subtree rooted at the given root node.
bool printAncestors(Node root, int node)
{
    // if tree is empty
    if (root == nullptr) {
        return false;
    }

    // TRUE if given node found
    if (root->data == node) {
        return true;
    }

    // search node in left subtree
    bool left = printAncestors(root->left, node);

    // search node in right subtree
    bool right = false;
    if (!left) {
        right = printAncestors(root->right, node);
    }

    // if given node found in either left or right subtree,
    // then current node is ancestor of a given node
    if (left || right) {
        print( root->data );
    }

    // if a node is found, return TRUE
    return left || right;
}
```

Pseudocode for iterative approach:

```
// Function to print root-to-leaf paths without using recursion
void rootToLeaf(unordered_map<int, int> parent, int key)
{
    while (key = parent[key]) {
        print( key );
    }

}

// Iterative function to set parent nodes for all nodes
// of the binary tree in a given map. The function is
// similar to the iterative preorder traversal
void setParent(Node root, unordered_map<int, int> &parent)
{
    // create an empty stack and push the root node
    stack<Node> stack;
    stack.push(root);

    // loop till stack is empty
    while (!stack.empty())
    {
        // Pop the top item from the stack
        Node* curr = stack.top();
        stack.pop();

        // push its right child into the stack and
        // set its parent on the map
        if (curr->right)
        {
            parent[curr->right->data] = curr->data;
            stack.push(curr->right);
        }

        // push its left child into the stack and set
        // its parent on the map
        if (curr->left)
        {
            parent[curr->left->data] = curr->data;
            stack.push(curr->left);
        }
    }
}

// Iterative function to print all ancestors of a given
```

123

```
// node in a binary tree
void printAncestors(Node root, int node)
{
    // base case
    if (root == nullptr) {
        return;
    }

    // create an empty map to store parent pointers of
    // binary tree nodes
    unordered_map<int, int> parent;

    // set the parent of the root node as 0
    parent[root->data] = 0;

    // set parent nodes for all nodes of the binary tree
    setParent(root, parent);

    // print ancestors of a given node using the parent map
    rootToLeaf(parent, node);
}
```

Space and Time complexity analysis

The time complexity of both recursive and iterative solution is O(N) where N represents the number of nodes in the binary tree.

For space complexity, the recursive solution does not require any extra space to store the nodes but requires space in the call stack (since recursion uses up the call stack). This extra space is equal to the height of the binary tree. Thus, the space complexity of the recursive solution is O(h) where h is the height of binary tree.

In the iterative solution, we use an explicit map to store all the nodes in the binary tree. As there are N nodes in the binary tree, the space complexity of the iterative solution is O(N).

Insight:

This problem may seem simple at first sight, but this brings in a key idea of using the current node to find properties of nodes that come before it. This is distinct from a simple traversal that we keep going deeper into the Binary Tree.

This understanding will help in solving some key problems of Binary Tree.

Largest Independent Set in Binary Tree

Given a Binary Tree, we have to find the size of Largest Independent Set (LIS) in it. A subset of all tree nodes is an independent set if there is no edge between any two nodes of the subset.

For example, consider the following binary tree. The largest independent set(LIS) is {1, 4, 8, 7, 5} and size of the LIS is 5.

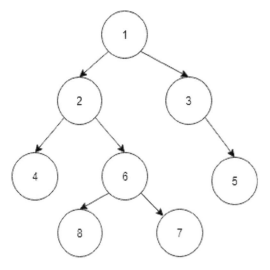

Basic approach

The most straightforward approach is to:

- Generate all subsets of nodes
- For each subset, check if it is independent and maintain the largest size

As there are N nodes, there will be 2^N subsets and for each subset, we need to do one traversal O(N) to check if it is independent. Hence, the time complexity of this approach will be **O(N x 2^N).**

This might seem easy to eliminate the N factor and bring the time complexity to $O(2^N)$ but going beyond it might look difficult.

126

In fact, this problem has an inherent structure within it and using a Dynamic Programming approach, we can solve it efficiently.

A Dynamic Programming solution solves a given problem using solutions of subproblems in bottom-up manner. Can the given problem be solved using solutions to subproblems? If yes, then what are the subproblems? Can we find largest independent set size (LISS) for a node X if we know LISS for all descendants of X? If a node is considered as part of LIS, then its children cannot be part of LIS, but its grandchildren can be. Following is optimal substructure property.

Let LISS(X) indicates size of largest independent set of a tree with root X.

```
LISS(X) = largest independent set with node X as root
```

The recursive structure is as follows:

```
LISS(X) = MAX { (1 + sum of LISS for all grandchildren of X),
                    (sum of LISS for all children of X) }
```

The idea is simple, there are two possibilities for every node X:

- either X is a member of the set
- X is not a member.

The implications are:

- If X is a member, then the value of LISS(X) is 1 plus LISS of all grandchildren.
- If X is not a member, then the value is sum of LISS of all children.

Following is recursive implementation that simply follows the recursive structure mentioned above.

```
// The function returns size of the
```

127

```
// largest independent set in a given
// binary tree
int LISS(node root)
{
        if (root == NULL)
        return 0;

        // Calculate size excluding the current node
        int size_excl = LISS(root->left) +
                        LISS(root->right);

        // Calculate size including the current node
        int size_incl = 1;
        if (root->left)
                size_incl += LISS(root->left->left) +
                                        LISS(root->left->right);
        if (root->right)
                size_incl += LISS(root->right->left) +
                                        LISS(root->right->right);

        // Return the maximum of two sizes
        return max(size_incl, size_excl);
}
```

Time complexity of the above naive recursive approach is exponential $O(2^N)$.

It should be noted that the above function computes the same subproblems again and again. Since same suproblems are called again, this problem has Overlapping Subprolems property. So LISS problem has both properties of a Dynamic programming problem. Like other typical Dynamic Programming (DP) problems, recomputations of same subproblems can be avoided by storing the solutions to subproblems and solving problems in bottom-up manner.

This Dynamic programming problem can be solved by **augmented tree** which means a modified tree structure. The augmented tree contain nodes having:

- data
- left child

128

- right child
- liss (an extra field)

Dynamic Programming Algorithm

The basic idea is as follows:

The size of largest independent set excluding root is the size for the left tree + right tree. This is because at this point it might not be clear that including root is compatible or not.

```
size excluding root = size(root->left) + size(root->right)
```

If we include the root, the minimum size is 1 and include the size of left node's children and right node's children. This is because left and right nodes cannot be included.

```
size including root = 1 + size(root->left->left) +
                  size(root->left->right) +
                  size(root->right->left) +
                  size(root->right->right)
```

Following is the pseudocode with the modified Binary Tree node definition:

```
/* A binary tree node has data, pointer
to left child and a pointer to
right child */
class node
{
        int data;
        int liss;
```

```
            node *left, *right;
};

// A memorization function returns size
// of the largest independent set in
// a given binary tree
int LISS(node root)
{
        if (root == NULL)
                return 0;

        if (root->liss)
                return root->liss;

        if (root->left == NULL && root->right == NULL)
                return (root->liss = 1);

        // Calculate size excluding the current node
        int liss_excl = LISS(root->left) + LISS(root->right);

        // Calculate size including the current node
        int liss_incl = 1;
        if (root->left)
                liss_incl += LISS(root->left->left) + LISS(root-
>left->right);
        if (root->right)
                liss_incl += LISS(root->right->left) + LISS(root-
>right->right);

        // Maximum of two sizes is LISS, store it for
        // future uses.
        root->liss = max(liss_incl, liss_excl);

        return root->liss;
}
```

Explanation

The idea is to maintain two list of alternative nodes that is grandchild nodes of
nodes. First go to the left most node of the tree and make the liss field of that node
is equal to one.

130

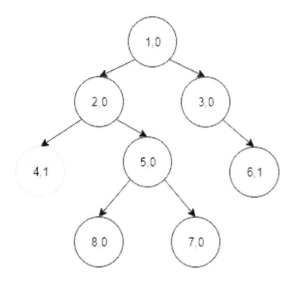

Then go to the right most node and the liss field of that node equal to one and liss_excl = 2.

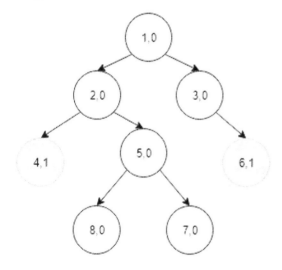

Now liss_incl = 1 and now go to another leaf node that is 8 and make the liss of that equal to one.

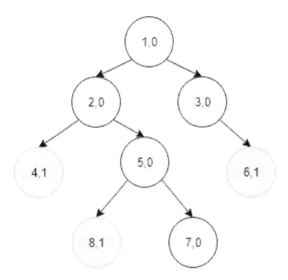

Then, go the right leaf node that is 7 and make liss of that equal to one and liss_incl=3.

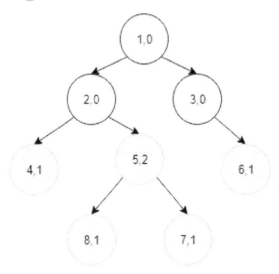

Then, go the parent and make its liss equal to liss_excl and liss_incl.

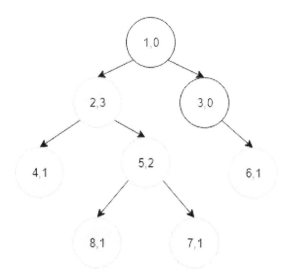

Now, assign the value of liss_incl to the parent.

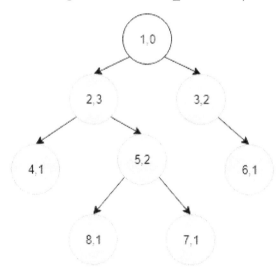

Now go the right of the root and assign its liss equal to one and liss_incl = 5 and assign root node liss equal to liss_incl.

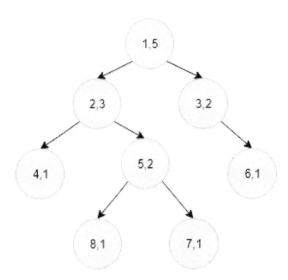

Hence, the answer is 5.

Time Complexity: O(N) where n is the number of nodes in given Binary tree.

Insight:

Observe that we identified a subset with a specific property with just one traversal and avoided going through all subsets. This is important as it brings in the idea that with just one traversal, we can extract a lot of information which can solve seemingly challenging problems.

Augmenting a data structure is yet another key idea where we need to tune a given structure to solve the problem efficiently.

Think about these ideas deeply.

134

Copy a binary tree where each node has a random pointer

We will explore algorithms to copy a binary tree with an additional pointer which points to any random node in the tree. This makes it challenging as a simple traversal will fail as the random pointer may point to a node which we have not yet encountered and hence, we will not be able to copy it.

Each node of the binary tree has following structure .

- key(value)
- left pointer
- right pointer
- random pointer

Random pointer can point to any random node of the binary tree or it can point to null.

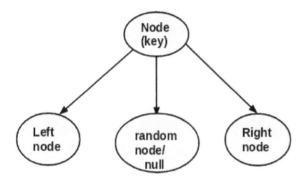

Example of a random pointer Binary tree:

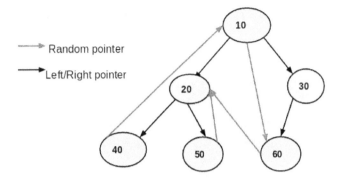

We will explore two techniques:

- Naive solution using 2 traversals
- Efficient solution using hashing

Naive solution: 2 traversals

The naive solution is to traverse the tree two times.

The first time we will traverse it using a standard traversal technique like inorder or preorder and use only the left and right pointers. This way we will copy the entire tree with every random pointer being null.

The idea of the second traversal is to fill up the random pointers. In the second traversal, we will go to each node using standard traversal techniques and copy the random pointer. For each random pointer, we need to find which node it corresponds to in the cloned Binary Tree which itself takes O(N) time.

At this point, we have copied the entire tree with 2 traversals.

The steps are:

- Clone Binary Tree with left and right child nodes
- Copy the random pointers [traverse through all N nodes]
  - For each random pointer, find the corresponding random node in the cloned Binary Tree [takes O(N) time]

Hence, the time complexity is $O(N^2)$ and space complexity is $O(1)$ not considering the space for cloned tree.

Efficient solution: Hashing

To copy a binary tree with random pointer, the effective solution is hashing.

We can copy binary tree by maintain a hash table for each node of given binary tree. This makes the time to figure out the corresponding random node in O(1) time instead of O(N) time.

Steps to copy binary tree using random pointer:

- Create a map to store mappings from a node to its clone
- Recursively traverse the binary tree. store key,left and right pointer of each node into hash table.

```
copynode.key    = treenode.key
copynode.left   = treenode.left
copynode.right  = treenode.right
map[treenode]   = clonenode
```

- update random pointers from the original binary tree into the map

```
copynode.random  =  map[treenode].random
```

The pseudocode is as follows:

```
// Copy function: calls 2 functions
// one to copy left and right child nodes
// other to copy random nodes
Node copytree(Node root)
{
    if (root == null)
        return null;

    // Hash Map
    Map<Node,Node> m=new HashMap();

    Node newtree = copyleftrightpointer(root,m);
```

137

```
      copyrandompointer(root,newtree,m);
      return newtree;
}

// Copy left and right pointers
Node copyleftrightpointer(Node treenode,Map<Node,Node>m)
{
   if (treenode == null)
      return null;

   // Create the copy node
   Node copynode=new Node(treenode.data);
   // Add entry in the Hash Map
   m.put(treenode, copynode);

   copynode.left  = copyleftrightpointer(treenode.left,m);
   copynode.right = copyleftrightpointer(treenode.right,m);
   return copynode;
}

// Copy random pointers
void copyrandompointer(Node treenode,Node
copynode,Map<Node,Node>m)
{
   if (copynode==null)
      return;

   copynode.random = m.get(treenode.random);
   copyrandompointer(treenode.left,copynode.left,m);
   copyrandompointer(treenode.right,copynode.right,m);
}
```

Code Explanation:

Original tree

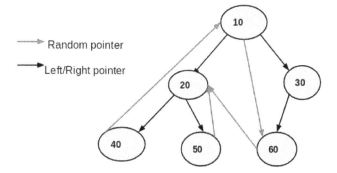

First, we create map to store mappings from node in the original tree to the corresponding node in the cloned tree.

Following this, we call the copyleftrightpointer() function which is a simple traversal like inorder traversal and does two things:

- Copies left and right child pointers of all nodes and creates the initial cloned tree
- Stores the mapping for each node in the map

Following this, we call copyrandompointer() function which is same as copyleftrightpointer() with some differences like:

- It copies the random pointer only.
- For the corresponding node, it uses the entries in the map.

With this, the Binary Tree is cloned.

Time complexity of above approach using hash map is O(N).

We do 2 traversals which take O(N) time each and finding corresponding nodes from hash map takes constant O(1) time.

The space complexity is O(N) for maintaining the hash map.

Insight:

There are other approaches to tackle this problem of which one is to modify the original Binary Tree (or create a copy with the modified structure) and following this, the clone of the original Binary Tree can be created using just one traversal.

If you notice carefully, we are still doing 2 traversals as one traversal is needed to modify the original Binary Tree. In terms of space, we do not get any advantage as well as we need to store the modified Binary Tree.

Think about this deeply.

Serialization and Deserialization of Binary Tree

The idea of Serialization and Deserialization of Binary Tree is that we convert a Binary Tree into a compressed form which can be saved in a file and retrieved back.

Serialization is the process of converting the object into bits. This makes it possible to store it in a memory buffer or a file. After serialization, the bits can be transmitted via signals over computers and networks.

On the other hand, Deserialization is the reverse of Serialization. It converts those bits back to the binary tree. When we serialize a binary tree, one thing must be kept in mind to maintain its correct structure.

To proceed with this, the key ideas are:

- Serialization of an array is a key process
- Binary Tree can be converted into an array using traversal techniques like inorder or preorder.
- If we have inorder and preorder traversal of a Binary Tree, then we can recreate the original Binary Tree.
- Once Binary Tree is converted into an array, the ideas of serialization of array can be used.

How can we serialize an array?

Serialization of the array is one of the basic operations that can be done.

To serialize an array, we can append the length of the array followed by some delimiter. The length will help us deserialize it in future for removal of the delimiter. So, we start with the length of the element followed by a delimiter and the element.

Example of Serialization of Array:

```
// Function to serialize a string array
string arrayserialize(string s[], int l)
{
    string t = "";
    for (int i=0; i<l; i++)
    {
        int l = s[i].length();
        t.push_back('0' + l);
        t = t + "-" + s[i];
    }
    return t;
}
```

In the above code snippet, we declare an empty string t. Then using for loop, we add the length of string to "l" and push that value to string "t". Then, we add delimiter or character (here "-") and the string to temp.

So, if the initial string is Opengenus, it would become 09-Opengenus.

If there is an array of 2 elements say ["OpenGenus", "Open"], then the serialized value will be **09-OpenGenus04-Open**

In deserialization of array, we will get the length inserted at starting of string. Then after the length from second letter onwards, traverse the letters mentioned in length. When we encounter a delimiter return the stored string and repeat the same process.

Example of Deserialization of Array:

```
void deserializearray(string s, string d[], int l)
{
    int length, position=0;
    string t = "";
    int i = 0;
    while(position>-1)
    {
        position = s.find("-", position+1);
```

142

```
        if(position>0)
        {
                length = s[position-1] - 48;
                t.append(s, position+1, length);
                d[i++] = t;
                t = "";
        }
    }
}
```

We start by initializing position with 0 and declaring length variable and an empty string t. Then we use while loop to iterate from the element next to "-" in array. If the position is returned greater than 0 then we store the length of string that lies on previous index of "-". We subtracted 48 because '6' has the int value 54

If we write '6'-'0' it evaluates to 54-48, or the int 6.

Now, we append "t" with "s" from position + 1 till length of string. Then, store the string t in d array. Now, initialize the string t as empty for next iteration.

Note: There are other elegant ways to serialize and deserialize an array and the approach we present is just for giving you the overall idea. It works equally well as other approaches.

The process of serialization and deserialization of a Binary Tree is as follows:

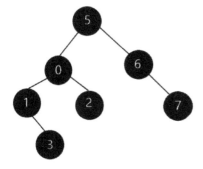

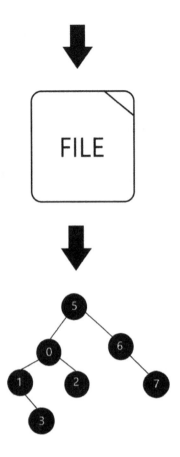

If the given tree is Binary Search Tree, then we can use preorder and postorder traversals to store it. For a general Binary Tree, we can use either of preorder or postorder traversal along with inorder traversal.

In case of Binary Tree is complete then level order traversal will be sufficient as all levels of the tree will be completely filled.

If given tree is Full Binary Tree, then every node will have either 0 or 2 children. Hence, preorder traversal will do along with storing a bit with every node to show if its internal or leaf node.

The process of serialization should be:

1. Get preorder traversal of the Binary Tree

2. Get inorder traversal of the Binary Tree
3. Serialize the two arrays from step 1 and 2 and save it

For deserialization, the process will be:

1. Deserialize the two arrays
2. Generate the Binary Tree from the inorder and preorder traversal
3. We have the final Binary Tree.

For special cases, we can use a simple approach like converting a Binary Tree to an array using preorder traversal and append the element with space as a delimiter. This will give you a clear idea of the overall process.

We will use preorder traversal to present the idea and mark Null pointers:

For Serialization:

```
// Encodes a tree to a single string.
string serialize(NODE root)
{
    stringstream ss;
    Helper(ss, root);
    return ss.str();
}

void Helper(STRING ss, NODE cur)
{
    if (!cur)
    {
        ss << "# ";
        return;
    }

    ss << cur->val + " ";

    Helper(ss, cur->left);
    Helper(ss, cur->right);
}
```

For deserialization:

```
// Decodes your encoded data to tree.
node* deserialize(string data)
{
    stringstream ss(data);
    node* root = nullptr;
    Helper(ss, root);
    return root;
}

void Helper(stringstream& ss, node* &cur)
{
    string Node;
    ss >> Node;
    if (Node == "" || Node == "#") {
        cur = nullptr;
        return;
    }

    stringstream sss(Node);
    int data;
    sss >> data;
    cur = new node();
    cur->val = data;
    cur->left = cur->right = nullptr;
    Helper(ss, cur->left);
    Helper(ss, cur->right);
}
```

In above approaches, we used the preorder traversal and marked the null as "#" after converting the tree to single string.

Recursive Approach:

Serialization Function

We can implement the serialize function as follows:

```
string emp = "X";
void serializeRecursive(node* root, ostringstream &os)
```

146

```
{
    if (root == nullptr)
    {
        os << emp << " ";
        return;
    }
    os << root->val;
    os << " ";
    serialize(root->left, os);
    serialize(root->right, os);
}

//Encoding tree to a single string
string serialize(node* root)
{
    ostringstream oss;
    serializeRecursive(root, oss);
    return oss.str();
}
```

Explanation:

Firstly, we initialize a string emp with "X".

Then, we have two functions, serialize and serializeRecursive.

The serialize function calls the serializeRecursive function iteratively.

Inside the serialize function, we create an output stream "oss".

Then we call the serializeRecursive function with root and oss as arguments.

Inside serializeRecursive function:

The base condition is if the root is null, the output string will emp, having value "X" to denote null node.

If the node is not null, then we insert the value of root into output string and empty string for the space between two consecutive node values.

Then, we recursively call the serializeRecurive function for traversing all the nodes of the left subtree.

147

Similarly, then we recursively call the serializeRecurive function for traversing all the nodes of the right subtree.

Once, the whole recurisve process is over, we return back to our Serialize function. Now, we return the output string "oss" as a string.

Deserialization Function

We can implement the deserialise function as follows:

```
node * deserializeRecursive(istringstream &is)
{
        string val;
        is >> val;
        if (val == emp)
        {
            return nullptr;
        }
        node *root = new node(stoi(val));
        root->left = deserialize(is);
        root->right = deserialize(is);
        return root;
}

// Decoding your encoded data to tree
node* deserialize(string data)
{
        istringstream is(data);
        return deserializeRecursive(is);
}
```

Explanation:

Firstly, we have two functions deserialize and deserializeRecursive.

Then, we have istringstream is(data), we pass the data in the input string stream to handle the input strings.

Then we return deserialization function by passing "is" that contains the data of input string stream.

Inside the deserializeRecurisve function:

148

Firstly, initialise the string val. Then, put it in input stream.

Whenever, the val is equivalent to emp (that is "X", representing the null node), we return the nullptr. It is the base condition.

If we do not have our base condition as true then the recursive function allocates the memory for a new node.

Similarly, we recursively iterate and reconstruct our binary tree by initializing values to our nodes. First, we call the function for left subtree and then for right subtree.

At the end we return out root.

Insight:

This may seem to be a simple problem, but this brings in a key idea. Any data structure how complex the structure is can be represented as a single dimensional data like an array or just an element and can be stored in a file.

This allows you to implement a hash function that can generate a hash for a Binary Tree. The idea is to create a serialized version and create a hash out of it.

0-1 Encoding of Binary Tree

Succinct encoding is an approach to convert a Binary Tree to a string or list of numbers with the lowest possible space and maintain the structural information. Based on the encoded string, we can recreate the structure of the original Binary Tree.

For example, if the Binary Tree is:

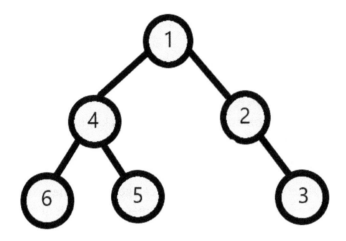

Then, this can be encoded as: **1 1 1 0 0 1 0 0 1 0 1 0 0**

There can be order encodings and this is one of the possible techniques. We will present the approach and then, you will be able to understand it effectively.

Number of different Binary Trees

The number of structurally different binary trees on N nodes is the Nth Catalan Number. Catalan numbers are a sequence of natural numbers that occur in various problems like counting the possible Binary Search trees with n values, counting the number of binary trees with n+1 leaves etc. Some Catalan numbers for n = 0, 1, 2, 3 ... are 1, 1, 2, 5 ...

Catalan Number C_i can be found using following formula:

150

$$C_0 = 1 \text{ and } C_{n+1} = \sum_{i=0}^{n} C_i \ C_{n-i} \text{ for all } n \geq 0$$

For large N, it becomes equivalent to 4 raised to power n ($C_N \sim 4^N$). Hence, we need at least log base 2 (4 raised to power n) bits to encode that.

Minimum bits: $\log_2(4^N) = \log_2(2^{2N}) = 2N$

It is equivalent to 2N. On the whole, a succinct tree would occupy 2N or O(N) bits to encode a Binary Tree with N nodes.

Encoding approach

To implement this encoding, we can first traverse the nodes of the tree in preorder traversal. This should output the encoding of "1" for internal node and "0" for leaf nodes. In case of the tree nodes containing values, we can store them in an array using preorder traversal.

Example:

For the below given tree,

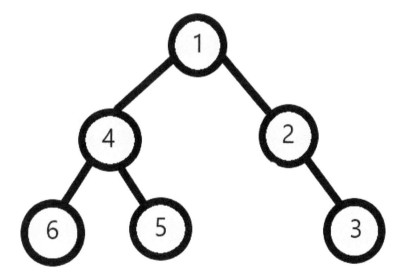

The preorder traversal will be: 1 4 6 5 2 3

If we consider NULL nodes, preorder traversal will be: 1 4 6 NULL NULL 5 NULL NULL 2 NULL 3 NULL NULL

Encoding will be: 1 1 1 0 0 1 0 0 1 0 1 0 0

Note: We changed the nodes to 1 and NULL nodes to 0.

We will check if the node is null. Since the root node is not null, then we append value of binary tree to data array and the value 1 as encoded value.

Then we go to left subtree.

So, after root node we check node 4. Since it is not null, hence we put 1 in encoding.

Then we check its left subtree. Node 6 is not null hence we put 1 in encoding. Then the left subtree of 6 is null hence we put 0. Then we check the right subtree of 6, which is null hence we again put 0.

Then we go back to node 4 and check right subtree of node 4. Node 5 is not null hence we insert 1. Then the left and right subtree of 5 is null hence we put 0. Then we return to node 4 then to node 1.

The left subtree of node 1 is traversed then we traverse the right subtree of node 1. Here the right subtree of node 1 is node 2. Hence, we insert 1. for the left subtree of node 2 we insert 0 and for the right subtree we have node 3.

For the node 3 we have both right and left subtree as null hence we insert 0. We kept on inserting the values of nodes in data array continuously.

We will have following encoding:

1 1 1 0 0 1 0 0 1 0 1 0 0

where 1 stand for data and 0 for NULL values.

Following the above algorithm, we can implement this problem as follows:

Algorithm for encoding

- Let us initialize s as the empty encoding string
- We start by checking if the node is null or not.
- If it is null, then we will append 0 to s.
- Else we append 1 to s.
- Then, we append value of node to data array at nth index.
- Then, we recursively call encoding function for left subtree and then for right subtree.

Following is the pseudocode for Encoding:

```
function encoding(node n, bitstring s, array data){
    if(n == NULL){
        append 0 to s;
    }
    else{
        append 1 to s;
        append n.data to data;
        encoding(n.left, s, data);
        encoding(n.right, s, data);
    }
}
```

Following is the implementation in C++ to give you an idea:

```
void encoding(node *root, list<bool> &s, list<int> data)
{
    if(root==0)
    {
        s.push_back(0);
```

153

```
        return;
    }
    else
    {
        s.push_back(1);
        data.push_back(root->val);
        encoding(root->left,s,data);
        encoding(root->right,s,data);
    }
}
```

Algorithm for decoding:

- We start by appending first bit of s to x and remove it from s
- If x is equivalent to 1 then we create new node n
- Then we remove first element of data and put in n.data
- We call recursively decoding function for left node and then for right node.
- Then we return n node.
- Else we return NULL

Example:

We have the following encoding given to us: **1 1 1 0 0 1 0 0 1 0 1 0 0**

For the decoding, since the first value is 1, hence we create new node.

The first element of data array be put in the value of the node. Hence, we obtain our root node with value 1. We follow this fashion for left nodes and then for right nodes. Then in the end we return node N and our tree is obtained. Else in the case of null node, we would return null.

Then, after the decoding we will get back our binary tree as below:

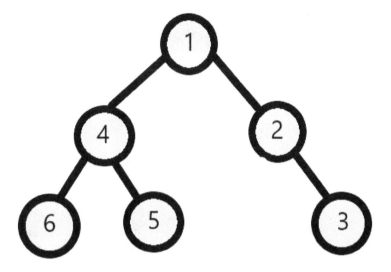

Following is the pseudocode of our decoding approach:

```
function decoding(bitstring s, array data)
{
    append first bit of s to x and remove it
    if(x==1)
    {
        create new node n
        remove first element of data and put in n.data
        n.left = decoding(s, data)
        n.right = decoding(s,data)
        return n
    }
    else
    {
        return null
    }
}
```

155

```
}
```

Following is the implementation of our decoding approach in C++:

```cpp
node *decoding(list<bool> &s, list<int> &data)
{
    if(s.size()==0)
        return NULL;
    else
    {
        bool b = s.front();
        s.pop_front();
        if(b==1)
        {
            int val = data.front();
            data.pop_front();
            node *root=newnode(val);
            root->left = decoding(s,data);
            root->right = decoding(s,data);
            return root;
        }
        return NULL;
    }
}
```

With the help of above functions, we can easily do encoding and decoding of the binary tree. We can use recursion for encoding and decoding of the tree as explained in above approaches.

Try these:

- Try to implement it as an iterative approach. This will be simple if you can implement preorder traversal iteratively.
- Try to use inorder and postorder traversal as well and see how the encoded string change for a given Binary Tree.

Insight:

This is important is cases when we need to reduce the storage of our Binary Tree to facilitate an intermediate process like transfer of data or make system memory available for a highly critical and memory heavy process.

ZigZag Traversal of Binary Tree

We have explored the 3 standard traversal techniques like Inorder, Preorder and Postorder. In fact, we can traverse a Binary Tree following several other rules and one type is **ZigZag traversal**.

The zigzag traversal of the binary tree can be better understood with an example. Consider the following Binary Tree:

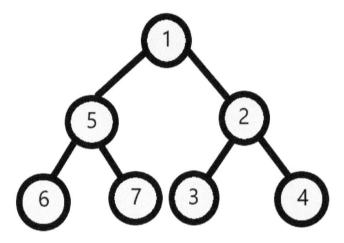

For the above tree, the zigzag traversal will be : **1 2 5 6 7 3 4**

Notice the traversal is left to right in i^{th} level and right to left in $i+1^{th}$ level alternatively.

There are many approaches for this problem like:

- **Approach 1:** We can use two stacks and swap the values of these stacks at each level.
- **Approach 2:** We can use deque to solve problem. Depending upon the even or odd level we will push or pop.
- **Approach 3:** We can also use recursion. It will print the spiral binary tree.
- **Approach 4:** Last approach will use iteration. We will use two stacks for printing left to right stack.

158

Approach 1

The problem can be solved using two stacks.

They could be *current* and **next**. There would be another variable required to keep track of current level order. We will print values of the nodes after popping from the left to right. Then we push the nodes left child, then its right child to the stack next. The stack is a LIFO structure, when we pop the nodes from the next, it will be reversed.

When current order is right to left then the nodes get pushed with right child first and then their left child. At the end of each level, we swap these stacks.

Algorithm:

- Firstly, we check if the root is null then we return else we move for next condition.
- We declare stack current and next.
- We push the root to current.
- Then we check if the stack is empty.
- If current is not empty, then we pop the top of current from stack. We store it in temp.
- If temp is not null then, we print the data in it.
- To store the data according to current order, we check if current node is left node or right node. According to them we push the data.
- If current is empty, then we swap current and next values.

Time Complexity: O(N)

Space Complexity: O(N) + O(N) = O(N)

Following is the implementation of approach 1 in C++:

```
void zigzag(struct node* root)
{
    if (!root)
```

```
        return;
    stack<struct node*> current;
    stack<struct node*> next;
    current.push(root);
    bool lefttoright = true;
    while (!current.empty()) {
        struct node* temp = current.top();
        current.pop();
        if (temp) {
            cout << temp->data << " ";
            if (lefttoright) {
                if (temp->left)
                    next.push(temp->left);
                if (temp->right)
                    next.push(temp->right);
            }
            else {
                if (temp->right)
                    next.push(temp->right);
                if (temp->left)
                    next.push(temp->left);
            }
        }
        if (current.empty()) {
            lefttoright = !lefttoright;
            swap(current, next);
        }
    }
}
```

Approach 2

This approach uses a *deque* to solve problem. Deque is double ended Queue (FIFO: First In First Out) data structure.

Depending upon the even or odd level we will push or pop.

We start the solution from level 1.

We start a loop till the queue is empty, we will pop the values from it if the level is even.

When level is odd then if the temp is left then we push value in q, and push value of node in v.

If temp is right, then we push the right node of temp in q and its value in v.

We will keep incrementing the level till the loop stops.

At the end, we return v.

Following is the implementation of Approach 2 in C++:

```cpp
vector<int> zigzag(node* root)
{
    deque<node*> q;
    vector<int> v;
    q.push_back(root);
    v.push_back(root->data);
    node* temp;
    int l = 1; //level
    while (!q.empty()) {
        int n = q.size();
        for (int i = 0; i < n; i++) {
            if (l % 2 == 0) {
                temp = q.back();
                q.pop_back();
            }
            else {
                temp = q.front();
                q.pop_front();
            }
            if (l % 2 != 0) {
            if (temp->right) {
                q.push_back(temp->right);
                v.push_back(temp->right->data);
            }
            if (temp->left) {
                q.push_back(temp->left);
                v.push_back(temp->left->data);
            }
        }
        else if (l % 2 == 0) {
            if (temp->left) {
```

```
                    q.push_front(temp->left);
                    v.push_back(temp->left->data);
                }
                if (temp->right) {
                    q.push_front(temp->right);
                    v.push_back(temp->right->data);
                }
            }
        }
        l++;
    }
    return v;
}
```

Approach 3:

In this approach we use recursion. It will print the binary tree in a spiral way.

We will print the nodes in different levels in iterating order.

We use a bool variable to change printing order of levels.

If itr is equivalent to 1, then we print nodes left to right.

Else we print nodes right to left.

We will complement value of bool variable in each iteration to change order.

We will use three functions in this approach:

- function level
- function height
- function zig zag

We will use level function to print nodes at various levels in tree. Function height will be used to check height of the tree and function zigzag we will print the zigzag traversal result.

Function Level in C++:

162

```
void Level(struct node* root, int level, int l)
{
    if (root == NULL)
        return;
    if (level == 1)
        cout << root->data << " ";
else if (level > 1)
    {
        if (l)
        {
            Level(root->left,level - 1, 1);
            Level(root->right,level - 1, 1);
        }
        else
        {
            Level(root->right,level - 1, 1);
            Level(root->left,level - 1, 1);
        }
    }
}
```

Function height:

In this function we will check the height of a tree.

We start by checking if the node is null. If so, then we return 0.

Else we compute the height of each subtree. In recursive fashion, we iterate the call left and right subtree.

Then we check if left height is greater or right subtree height. We return the greater height + 1.

Following is the implementation of height function in C++:

```
int height(struct node* node)
{
    if (node == NULL)
        return 0;
```

163

```
    else
    {
        int left = height(node->left);
        int right = height(node->right);
        if (left > right)
            return (left + 1);
        else
            return (right + 1);
    }
}
```

Function zigzag:

In this function, we will print the zigzag traversal result. We initialize the height of tree using height function defined above.

Then we initialize boolean "ltr" with false.

Then we have for loop from 1 till height of tree. Here we call the Level function defined above in each iteration.

We also revert "ltr" to traverse next level in opposite order.

Following is the implementation of zigzag function in C++:

```
void zigzag(struct node* root)
{
    int h = height(root);
    int i;
    bool ltr = false;
    for(i = 1; i <= h; i++)
    {
        Level(root, i, ltr);
        ltr = !ltr;
    }
}
```

Time complexity is: $O(N^2)$.

The skewed trees give worst cases.

Approach 4

This is the iterative approach. We will use two stacks for printing left to right stack.

We use two stacks one for left to right and other for right to left.

In each iteration, we have nodes of one level in one of the stacks.

We will print nodes, and then push nodes of next level in the other stack.

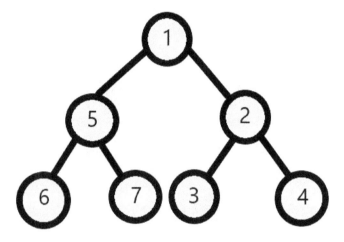

For the above tree, we check if the root is null or not. Since in the above tree it is not the case, we initialize s1 and s2 stack. Then we push the root to s1 stack.

Now, we start iteration till s1 or s2 is not empty. Then, we have another while loop within it. It will iterate till s1 is not empty. Then we have temp that will store the top node of s1. Which right now will be the root node. Then we pop the root node from the s1 stack and print the data of root node. If the right of the root node is not null, then s2 will store the value temp. If the left of node is not null then we will store its value in s2.

This will store values for right to left.

Then we will enter another loop where we start by initializing value of top of s2 in temp. Then we pop top value of s2 and print its data. If the left of temp node is not

165

null, then we will store its value in s1. Then if the right of temp is not null then we will store its value in right of temp.

This will store values for left to right.

Following is the implementation of spiral function in C++:

```cpp
void spiral(struct node* root)
{
    if (root == NULL)
        return;
    stack<struct node*> s1;
    stack<struct node*> s2;
    s1.push(root);
    while (!s1.empty() || !s2.empty()) {
        while (!s1.empty()) {
            struct node* temp = s1.top();
            s1.pop();
            cout << temp->data << " ";
            if (temp->right)
                s2.push(temp->right);
            if (temp->left)
                s2.push(temp->left);
        }
        while (!s2.empty()) {
            struct node* temp = s2.top();
            s2.pop();
            cout << temp->data << " ";
            if (temp->left)
                s1.push(temp->left);
            if (temp->right)
                s1.push(temp->right);
        }
    }
}
```

Therefore, we can opt for any of the above approaches to find the zig zag manner of the tree. We can use stacks with complexity O(N), or we can use the deque approach, or the recursion approach or the iterative approach.

166

Each of them will give us zig zag binary tree from the given binary tree.

Insight:

This is an important problem as it reminds us that we can do traversal in any way we want. Each traversal comes with its own properties and hence, using the right traversal technique is the key to solve a problem efficiently.

Can you think of other ways we can traverse a Binary Tree?

Check if 2 Binary Trees are isomorphic

Two Binary Trees are known to be isomorphic if one of them can be obtained from the other one by series of flipping of nodes that is swapping the children both left and right of number of nodes. Any number of nodes at all levels can swap their child nodes.

With above definition we can say that two empty trees are isomorphic.

Let us consider an example:

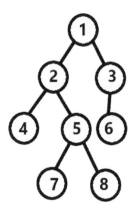 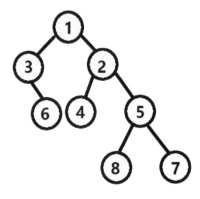

Above trees are isomorphic.

We can swap node 2 and 3. Then we can swap node NULL and 6. Then finally we can swap node 7 and 8.

We have two main approaches to follow:

- In approach 1, we need to traverse both trees first.
- In approach 2, we will traverse the trees iteratively using level order traversal and store that in a queue. At each level we will iterate through array to check whether each value exist on map or not.

Approach 1

168

We need to traverse both trees first. Let current internal nodes of two trees being traversed be n1 and n2.

To be isomorphic we have following conditions:

- Data of n1 is equivalent to n2
- One of following is true for children of n1 and n2:
- Left child of n1 is isomorphic to left child of n2.
- Right child of n1 is isomorphic to right child of n2
- Left child of n1 is isomorphic to right child of n2
- Right child of n1 is isomorphic to left child of n2

Consider the following two Binary Trees:

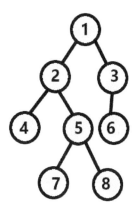 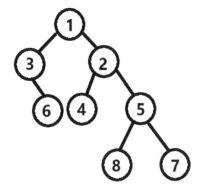

For the above tree, we start by checking if roots of both trees are null.

Since roots of both trees are not null, we check the condition if the value of both root nodes of both trees is equal. Since the value of both root nodes is same, we return the iterative call of function Isomorphic.

First, we will check the condition if left child of both trees is isomorphic and the right child of nodes of both trees are isomorphic. If any of these conditions holds true, then the result will be false since they have && operator.

Second, in "or" operator we called the function again for left and right child of both trees. Using && operator to this condition, we check for right and left child nodes.

169

Now, the left and right child node of first tree is 2 and 3, respectively. The left and right child node of second tree is 3 and 2, respectively.

For the first recursive call, we have left child node of first and second tree. Since both of them have different values. Hence this will result in false.

For the second recursive call we have right child node of first and second tree. They both again have different values. Hence it returns false.

For the third recursive call, we have left and right child nodes of first and second tree, respectively. It returns true.

For the fourth recursive call, we have right and left child nodes of first and second tree, respectively. It returns true.

Hence the overall result will be true. In similar fashion we will keep traversing whole tree and find out if it is isomorphic or not.

Function Isomorphic:

- In the function we start by checking if both roots are null or not. If they are null, then the trees are isomorphic. Hence, we return true if so.

- Then we check if one of n1 and n2 are null then the trees are not isomorphic.

- Then we start to check for both trees being isomorphic if none of above conditions hold true:

    - We start a loop till value of n1 is not equivalent to value of n2

    - We call the Isomorphic function recursively to check :

        - The subtree rooted at these nodes have not been flipped, both of these subtrees have to be isomorphic

        - The subtrees rooted at these nodes have been flipped

Following is the pseudocode of the above approach:

170

```
bool Isomorphic(node* n1, node *n2)
{
    if (n1 == NULL && n2 == NULL)
        return true;
    if (n1 == NULL || n2 == NULL)
        return false;
    if (n1->val != n2->val)
        return false;
    return
        (Isomorphic(n1->left,n2->left) &&
        Isomorphic(n1->right,n2->right)) ||
        Isomorphic(n1->left,n2->right) &&
        Isomorphic(n1->right,n2->left));
}
```

This solution will take Time Complexity of **O(min(x,y) * 2) or O(min(x,y))** where x and y represent the number of nodes in given trees.

Approach 2

We will traverse the trees iteratively using level order traversal and store that in a queue. The conditions to be checked are:

- The values of nodes are same
- The number of nodes at each level is same

We have to check the size of queue to ensure that the second condition is true. We will store the nodes of each level of first tree as val. For second tree store the nodes of the tree in vector. In case of repetitive values, we will decrease the value to keep track of how many nodes with same value exist at given level. If value become zero, then it shows that the first tree only has this number of nodes. At each level we will iterate through array to check whether each value exist on map or not. There are 3 key conditions:

- If the key is not found, then first tree does not have node found in other tree does not have node at given level.
- If key is found but value is negative, then second tree has more nodes with same value as first one.

- If size of the map is not zero, then it means there are some keys left. Hence the first tree has node that does not match any node in other tree.

Function Isomorphic:

- We check if both roots are null, then the tree is isomorphic

- Else we check if one node is false

- Then we start to enqueue the roots of both trees if above conditions are false

- Then we start a while loop till either queue is empty

    - We check if number of nodes are not same at given level

    - Then in another loop we dequeue the nodes

    - We check if the value exists in the map

    - Then we enqueue the child nodes

- Then we iterate through each node to check if it exists. We do this at each level

- Finally, we check if there is any key remaining then we return false

- Else return true

Following is the implementation of our approach in Python:

```
bool Isomorphic(node* root1, node* root2)
{
    if (root1 == NULL and root2 == NULL)
        return true;
    else if (root1 == NULL or root2 == NULL)
        return false;
        queue<node *> q1, q2;
    q1.push(root1);
    q2.push(root2);
    int level = 0,size;
    vector<int> v2;
```

```cpp
        unordered_map<int, int> mp;
        while (!q1.empty() && !q2.empty()) {
            if (q1.size() != q2.size())
                return false;
            size = q1.size();
            level++;
            v2.clear();
            mp.clear();
            while (size--) {
                node* temp1 = q1.front();
                node* temp2 = q2.front();
                q1.pop();
                q2.pop();
                if (mp.find(temp1->data) == mp.end())
                    mp[temp1->data] = 1;
                else
                    mp[temp1->data]++;
                v2.push_back(temp2->data);
                if (temp1->left)
                    q1.push(temp1->left);
                if (temp1->right)
                    q1.push(temp1->right);
                if (temp2->left)
                    q2.push(temp2->left);

                if (temp2->right)
                    q2.push(temp2->right);
            }
            for (auto i : v2) {
                if (mp.find(i) == mp.end())
                    return false;
                else {
                    mp[i]--;
                    if (mp[i] < 0)
                        return false;
                    else if (mp[i] == 0)
                        mp.erase(i);
                }
            }
            if (mp.size() != 0)
                return false;
        }
    return true;
}
```

173

In second approach, we are traversing the trees iteratively using level order traversal and store that in a queue. Then we will check the mentioned conditions.

Hence, the time complexity is O(N + M) with space complexity of O(N+M).

N and M are number of nodes in the two Binary Trees, respectively.

Insight:

This might seem to be a standard problem, but this has applications in other fields like Chemistry. Many may associate the word "Isomorphic" to Chemistry and hence, the idea we explored is a fundamental concept in designing Algorithms for Computational Chemistry.

Can you use Binary Tree in other ideas like representing DNA and support features like Mutation? Try this.

Convert Binary Tree to Circular Doubly Linked list

In this problem, we will convert a Binary Tree to Circular Doubly Linked List. This is important as both are two distinct Data Structures.

To convert Binary Tree to Circular Doubly Linked List, we will take left node as previous pointer and right node as next pointer. The order of nodes in Doubly Linked List must be same as in inorder of the given binary tree.

The very first node of inorder traversal will become the head of the doubly linked list.

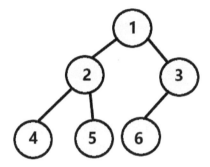

In the above binary tree, we will get the doubly linked list as follows:

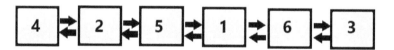

We need to check following conditions:

- If **left subtree exists**, then process left subtree to DLL. We will use recursion to convert left subtree to DLL. Then we will find inorder predecessor (left most node in left subtree) of root in left subtree. Then we will make inorder predecessor as previous of root.

- If **right subtree exists**, then we follow below conditions to process it. Recursively convert right subtree to DLL. Find inorder successor of root in right subtree. Make inorder successor as next of root. Make root as previous of inorder successor. Find leftmost node and return that as head of dll.

We have two main approaches:

- **In first approach**, we will use two functions: convert and dll function. We will use inorder traversal to convert the binary tree. We will form the doubly linked list by using the inorder traversal list.
- **In second approach**, we will traverse the tree in inorder fashion and keep track of each node we visit.

Approach 1

In this approach we will use two functions:

- convert function
- dll function

In convert function we will use inorder traversal to convert the binary tree. In next function, dll we will form the doubly linked list by using convert function.

Function convert:

In this we first check if the nodes are null or not.

Then we convert the left subtree and link it to the root. Then we will convert the left subtree.

Then we will find the inorder predecessor. After this loop, left points to the inorder predecessor.

Make root as next of predecessor and predecessor as previous of root.

Then, we convert right subtree and link it to the root.

Then, we will convert the right subtree.

176

Then, we will find the inorder successor. After the loop, right will point to the inorder successor.

Make root as previous of successor.

Make successor as next of root.

Following is the implementation of the convert function:

```
node* convert(node* root)
{
    if (root == NULL)
        return root;
    if (root->left != NULL) {
        node* left = bintree2listUtil(root->left);
        for (; left->right != NULL; left = left->right);
        left->right = root;
        root->left = left;
    }
    if (root->right != NULL) {
        node* right = bintree2listUtil(root->right);
        for (; right->left != NULL; right = right->left);
        right->left = root;
        root->right = right;
    }
    return root;
}
```

Function dll:

First, we check for the base case. If the root is null, then we return root.

Else, then we call convert function above. It returns the root node of converted DLL.

We will need pointer to left most node as it will be the head for the DLL. Now we start a while loop to return left most node.

In the end, we return root.

Following is the implementation of dll function:

```
node* dll(node* root)
{   if (root == NULL)
        return root;
    root = convert(root);
    while (root->left != NULL)
        root = root->left;
    return (root);
}
```

Approach 2:

In this approach, we will traverse the tree in inorder fashion. We will keep track of each node we visit. We will keep track of the DLL head and tail pointers, insert each visited node at end of DLL using tail ptr. Finally, we return the head of the list.

Following is the implementation of the convert function:

```
node* convert(node* root, node** head, node** tail)
{
    if (root == NULL)
        return NULL;
    node* left = root->left;
    node* right = root->right;
    convert(root->left, head, tail);
    if (*head == NULL) {
        *head = root;
    }
    root->left = *tail;
    if (*tail != NULL) {
        (*tail)->right = root;
    }
    *tail = root;
    convert(root->right, head, tail);
    return root;
}
```

Function dll:

Firstly, we check if the root is null. If so, then we return null.

Else we initialize head and tail pointers as null.

Then we call convert function.

In the end we return head.

Following is the implementation of dll function:

```
node* dll(node* root)
{
    if (root == NULL)
        return root;
    node* head = NULL;
    node* tail = NULL;
    convert(root, &head, &tail);
    return head;
}
```

Approach 3:

In this approach have two types of pointers:

- **Fixed Left pointers**: We will fix the left pointer. We will change left pointers to point to previous nodes in DLL. We will perform inorder traversal of the tree. In inorder traversal, we will keep track of previous visited nodes. We will change left pointer to previous node.
- **Fixed right pointers**: We will use the left pointers fixed as above. Starting from rightmost node in Binary Tree, it is the last node in DLL. Since left pointers are changed to point to previous node in DLL. Hence, we can traverse the complete DLL using these pointers. The traversal is from last to first node. While traversing we will keep track of previously visited node. We will change right pointer to previous node.

We have four main functions:

- In function Inorder we will do inorder traversal of binary tree.

179

- In function prev, we change left pointers to work as previous pointers. The function is performing inorder traversal.
- In function next, we change right pointers to act as next pointers in converted DLL.
- In function fin, we convert the binary tree to DLL.

Time Complexity : **O(N)**

Function Inorder:

This function implements the inorder traversal.

First, we check if the root is not null. Then, we recursively call this function for left subtree.

Then recursively we call this function for right subtree.

Following is the implementation in C++:

```cpp
void inorder(node *root)
{
    if (root != NULL)
    {
        inorder(root->left);
        cout << root->data;
        inorder(root->right);
    }
}
```

Function prev:

In this function, we change left pointers to work as previous pointers.

The function is performing inorder traversal.

Then it updates left pointer using previously visited node.

Following is the implementation in C++:

```cpp
void prev(node *root)
{
    static node *pre = NULL;
    if (root != NULL)
    {
        prev(root->left);
        root->left = pre;
        pre = root;
        prev(root->right);
    }
}
```

Function next:

In this function, we change right pointers to act as next pointers in converted DLL

We find the right most node in binary tree or last node in DLL

We start from the rightmost node, traverse using left pointers.

While traversing we change right pointer of nodes

The leftmost node is the head of the linked list. We will return it.

Following is the implementation in C++:

```cpp
node *next(node *root)
{
    node *prev = NULL;
    while (root && root->right != NULL)
        root = root->right;
    while (root && root->left != NULL)
    {
        prev = root;
        root = root->left;
        root->right = prev;
    }
    return (root);
```

181

```
}
```

Function fin:

In this function, we convert the binary tree to DLL.

We first set previous pointer.

Then we set next pointer and return head of DLL.

Then we traverse the DLL from left to right.

Following is the implementation in C++:

```cpp
node *fin(node *root)
{
    prev(root);
    return next(root);
}
void printList(node *root)
{
    while (root != NULL)
    {
        cout<<root->data;
        root = root->right;
    }
}
```

Approach 4:

It is the most optimal approach. Time Complexity is O(N).

In this approach, we will do inorder traversal of binary tree. While inorder traversal we will keep track of the previously visited nodes in prev variable. For each node that has been visited we make it next of prev and previous of this node as prev. Instead of static used in below implementation we can also use double pointer or reference pointer.

182

For example consider the below tree:

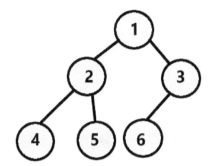

We start by checking if the root is null. Since this is not the case hence, we move to next condition. We initialize prev with NULL. Then we call convert function recursively for the left subtree of the root, starting from node 2. Then again, we would call left child of node 2, that is node 4. Then the node 4 will have no left child, hence we will return. Then since the prev will be NULL hence we initialize head with root, that is node 4. Prev will be set to node 4 that is root for this call. Then node 4 does not have right child node either. Hence, we return and now the root is node 2.

Now left of root will be prev that is node 4 and right of prev will be root that is node 2. Now the prev will be node 2. Then we will call the convert function for left subtree with root node 2.

In the same fashion we will keep making recursive calls and hence our doubly linked list would be formed in the end.

Function convert:

- We start by checking if the root is null. If so, then we return.
- Else Initialize the previously visited node as NULL.
- We have taken it static for accessibility of same value in all recursive calls.
- Then we recursively convert the left subtree
- Then we convert the node
- Then we convert the right subtree.

Following is the implementation in C++:

183

```
void convert(node *root, node **head)
{
    if (root == NULL) return;
    static node* prev = NULL;
    convert(root->left, head);
    if (prev == NULL)
        *head = root;
    else
    {
        root->left = prev;
        prev->right = root;
    }
    prev = root;
    convert(root->right, head);
}
```

Hence, using above approaches we can easily convert Binary Tree to Circular Doubly Linked list. We can either use inorder traversal as mentioned in approach 1 and 2. We can also use optimal approach consuming O(n) time complexity by using two fixed pointers. It will also use inorder traversal.

At the end we have the most optimal, approach 4 using O(n) with inorder traversal. Instead of static used in below implementation we can also use double pointer or reference pointer.

Insight:

If you observe carefully, all approaches are fundamentally same. This brings in the idea that some approaches are same but still performance and analysis may difference because the way we implement is important.

This does not mean that all approaches are same. There are distinct approaches and this results in different classes of problems which comes under Complexity Theory.

Introduction to Skewed Binary Tree

A binary tree can be called a skewed binary tree if all nodes have one child or no child at all. They can be of two types:

- Left Skewed Binary Tree
- Right Skewed Binary Tree

Left Skewed Binary Tree

If all nodes are having a left child or no child at all then, it can be called a left skewed binary tree. In this tree all children at right side remain null.

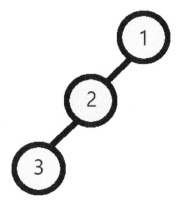

Right Skewed Binary Tree

If all nodes are having a right child or no child at all then it can be called a right skewed binary tree. In this tree all children at left side remain null.

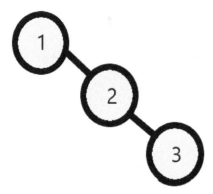

Case 1 : Left skewed binary tree

In case of left skewed binary tree, we will insert values only in left nodes and leave all right nodes as null.

```
node * root= newnode(5);
root->left = newnode(8);
root->left->left = newnode(10);
```

The above code snippet creates a new node, that will be the root for our tree and initialize it with value 5. Then, it creates its left node with value 8 and further its left node with value 10.

Case 2 : Right skewed binary tree

In case of right skewed binary tree, we will insert values only in right nodes and leave all left nodes as null.

```
node * root= newnode(5);
root->right = newnode(8);
root->right->right = newnode(10);
```

186

The above code snippet creates a new node, that will be the root for our tree and initialize it with value 5. Then, it creates its right node with value 8 and further its right node with value 10.

Note: A skewed Binary Tree is what we want to avoid in real problems as it reduces to an array and takes algorithms to their worst case. Still, we will analyze this structure and understand it so that we can handle this better.

Some specific problems require the use of Skewed Binary Tree for efficiency.

187

Check if Binary Tree is skewed or not

There are two types of skewed binary trees: Left and Right skewed binary trees. From their characteristics we can conclude that they either have one child node or no node at all.

Hence, below given binary tree is skewed.

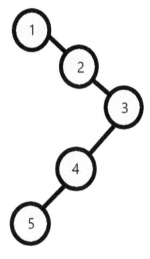

and below binary tree is not skewed since one of its nodes have two child nodes.

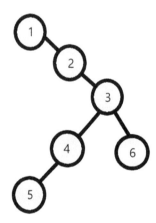

Hence, in its implementation we will recursively check if the nodes of the binary tree have one child nodes or no node. If so, then we will keep traversing else return false on encountering two child nodes.

Algorithmic Steps:

For each node N, check the following:

- If both left and right child nodes are present, it is not a valid skewed tree.
- If the node has only one left child node, then we check its left child node
- If the node has only one right child node, then we check its right child node
- If there are no child nodes, it is a valid node of a skewed tree.

The pseudocode is as follows:

```
skewed(node* root)
{
    //This condition checks if the given is null node or leaf node
    if (root == NULL || (root->left == NULL &&
                         root->right == NULL))
        return true;

    //Now, we check if the node has two children, if yes then we return false
    if (root->left && root->right)
        return false;

    //If the node has only one left child node then we check its left child node
    //else we check its right root node
    if (root->left)
        return skewed(root->left);
    return skewed(root->right);
}
```

Explanation:

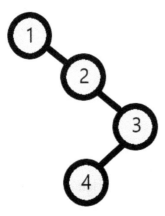

Consider the above binary tree. Firstly, the function will check if the root is null or if both left and right nodes are null. In above binary tree, initially this condition is false.

Now, it checks if the right and the left nodes are not null. If so, it will return false since skewed binary tree can only have one child either on left or right. In above binary tree it is not the case.

Now, we come for the last condition. If the left node is not null, then it returns recursively the left node of the root. Else, in similar recursive fashion it returns the right node of root.

This way in above example, the leaf node will satisfy first condition of null left and null right node and hence return true. Hence, it is a skewed binary tree.

If the tree would not have been skewed, then the function would have returned false.

Time Complexity

- **Best Case** : O(1) if the root has two children
- **Worst Case** : O(k) if the tree is skewed where k is the height of tree
- **Space Complexity**: O(1)

Insight:

190

By examining each node irrespective of the overall structure, we can identify if a Binary Tree is skewed. Hence, specific types depending on the structure of a Binary Tree does not depend on checking the overall structure. This is an important property.

Change Binary Tree to Skewed Binary Tree

A simple binary tree can be easily converted into a skewed binary tree. We know that a skewed binary tree can be of two types:

- Left Skewed Binary Tree
- Right Skewed Binary Tree

Hence, we can convert binary tree into two types of skewed binary trees provided we have Binary Search Trees:

- Increasing Skewed Binary Trees
- Decreasing Skewed Binary Trees

Consider a binary tree:

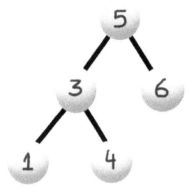

Case 1 : Increasing Order

We will do inorder traversal, as inorder traversal of a Binary Search Tree provides us increasing sequence of values of nodes.

Using above logic, the left node traversal will give us smaller values.

Then after traversal of left subtree, we will add previous node of skewed tree to our root node.

For the larger values, now we traverse the right subtree.

192

The Increasing skewed binary tree will be:

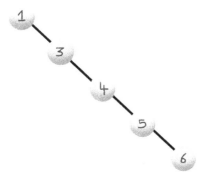

The overall steps are:

- Get the inorder traversal of the tree (that is the left most element in the Binary Tree)
- Insert new nodes as right child in the new Skewed Tree

For inorder traversal, we will do:

- right child node
- root node
- left child node

Hence, the steps are:

- Convert the right child sub-tree to skewed tree
- If head node is not set, set head node as the current root node.
- If head node is set, make the current root node as the right child of the previous node. (In implementation, you may handle head node and previous node as a common variable across function calls).
- Convert the left child sub-tree to skewed tree

This may be hard to realize at first. Think over the steps and you will realize how this is same as doing a simple inorder traversal.

Following is the pseudocode for Increasing order (case 1):

193

```
void skewed(node *root)
{
    // Base Case
    // headNode and prevNode are global variables
    if (!root)
        return;

    // To check the order in which the skewed tree should be made
    skewed(root->right);

    node *rightNode = root->right;
    node *leftNode = root->left;

    // To check if the root Node of the skewed tree is not
defined
    if (!headNode)
    {
        headNode = root;
        root->left = NULL;
        prevNode = root;
    }
    else
    {
        prevNode->right = root;
        root->left = NULL;
        prevNode = root;
    }

    // Now we will Recurse for the left or right subtree on the
basis of the order
    skewed(leftNode);
}
```

Case 2 : Decreasing Order

Recursion of the right node will be done first in order to get larger values first.

Then we will connect the root node after the previous node.

At the end we traverse the left subtree for smaller values since the tree should be skewed in decreasing order.

194

The decreasing skewed binary tree will be:

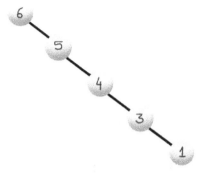

For inorder traversal, we will do:

- left child node
- root node
- right child node

Hence, the steps are:

- Convert the left child sub-tree to skewed tree
- If head node is not set, set head node as the current root node.
- If head node is set, make the current root node as the right child of the previous node. (In implementation, you may handle head node and previous node as a common variable across function calls).
- Convert the right child sub-tree to skewed tree

This may be hard to realize at first. Think over the steps and you will realize how this is same as doing a simple inorder traversal. If you understood the first case, then this is the same with the order reversed.

The pseudocode will be as follows:

```
void skewed(node *root)
{
    // Base Case
    if (!root)
        return;
```

195

```
    // To check the order in which the skewed tree should be made
    skewed(root->left);

    node *rightNode = root->right;
    node *leftNode = root->left;

    // To check if the root Node of the skewed tree is not
defined
    if (!headNode)
    {
        headNode = root;
        root->left = NULL;
        prevNode = root;
    }
    else
    {
        prevNode->right = root;
        root->left = NULL;
        prevNode = root;
    }

    // Now we will Recurse for the left or right subtree on the
basis of the order
    skewed(rightNode);
}
```

Both the functions for Increasing and Decreasing order can be merged together using a control variable K where:

- K = 1 for Increasing order
- K = 0 for Decreasing order

We have presented the merged function skewed(node, K) accordingly.

Final implementation can be done as follows:

```
void skewed(node *root, int k)
{
    // Base Case
```

196

```
    if (!root)
        return;

    // To check the order in which the skewed tree should be made
    if (k)
        skewed(root->right, k);
    else
        skewed(root->left, k);

    node *rightNode = root->right;
    node *leftNode = root->left;

    // To check if the root Node of the skewed tree is not
defined
    if (!headNode)
    {
        headNode = root;
        root->left = NULL;
        prevNode = root;
    }
    else
    {
        prevNode->right = root;
        root->left = NULL;
        prevNode = root;
    }

    // Now we will Recurse for the left or right subtree on the
basis of the order
    if (k)
        skewed(leftNode, k);
    else
        skewed(rightNode, k);
}
```

Explanation:

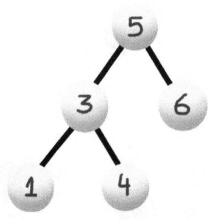

In above tree, the function will start by checking if root is null. If so, then it will return. This is not the case with our example.

If k is 1, that means we need to follow increasing order. Hence, we will recursively call the right child of root and pass k as argument to keep the track if we need to find increasing or decreasing order of skewed binary tree.

Then, we make a new node for the final skewed tree. We initialize the left node with left child of root and right with right child of node.

If the root of the skewed binary tree is not defined, then we define the head node and right node of skewed tree as root. The left node is defined null since it is a skewed binary tree, and it can only have one child.

If head node is already defined then the right child of previous node is given value of our root and left child is null since in skewed tree, one node can have only one child. Previous node is given value of root.

At the end we recurse according to our value of k that defines if the order will be increasing or decreasing.

If k is 1 then we recursively call function and pass left node as argument else we will pass right node if k = 0.

Time Complexity: O(N) as we traverse through the tree only once.

Space Complexity: O(N) in a recursive implementation due to function call stack.

Insight:

This problem is important as it illustrates how we can generate a new structure just by going through the traversal the first time. At first, it seems that the problem requires information of the entire traversal, but it is not true as evident by our algorithm.

Can you think of other information that can be generated while going through the traversal?

Threaded Binary Tree

Threaded Binary Tree is a binary tree with an additional property that null pointers of leaf node of the binary tree is set to inorder predecessor or inorder successor (that is the predecessor and successor as in an inorder traversal).

The main idea behind setting such a structure is to make the inorder and preorder traversal of the tree faster without using any additional data structure (like auxiliary stack) or memory to do the traversal. This is useful in small systems where hardware is very limited, so we use threaded binary tree for better efficiency of the software in a limited hardware space.

Types of Threaded Binary Tree

There are two types of threaded binary tree:

- Single Threaded Binary Tree
- Double Threaded Binary Tree

Single Threaded Binary Tree: In this case, only the right NULL pointer is made to point to inorder successor.

Double Threaded Binary Tree: In this case, both the right as well as the left NULL pointers are made to point inorder successor and inorder predecessor respectively. (the left threads are helpful in reverse inorder traveral of the tree)

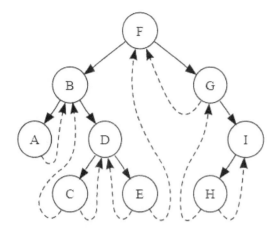

Double Threaded Binary Tree

Structure of node in threaded binary tree

A node in threaded binary tree has two additional attributes:

- rightThread
- leftThread

Both new attributes are of type Boolean.

Following is the node structure in a Single threaded binary tree and Double threaded binary tree:

```
// single threaded

class Node
{
    int data ;
    Node left ;
    Node right ;
    bool rightThread ;
}

// double threaded
```

201

```
class Node
{
    int data ;
    Node left ;
    Node right ;
    bool leftThread ;
    bool rightThread ;
}
```

Significance of bool variable (leftThread and rightThread) in structure

If we have some address stored in some node to differentiate whether that address is of parent node or of child node, we use leftThread and rightThread bool variables.

leftThread and rightThread bool variables stores whether left and right pointers point to child node or some ancestor node , if the bool variable is set to true that means pointer is pointing to child node and if it is set to 1 that means that pointer is pointing to parent node.

For example:

Let us say for some node right pointer is pointing to some node and righThread is set to true, this means that it is pointing to a child node but if in the same case, if rightThread is set to false this means that it is pointing to a parent node (and not child node).

What happens with rightmost and leftmost null nodes ?

When we create a threaded binary tree the left most and rightmost pointers do not have inorder predecessor or inorder successor so they are made to point to a dummy node (as you can see in the previous image) and leftThread of leftmost node and rightThread of rightmost node is set to false.

Operations in Threaded Binary Tree

202

We can also perform various operations in a threaded binary tree like:

1. Insert

2. Search

3. Delete

After performing the above operations, we need to make sure that our new binary tree still follows all the conditions of a threaded binary tree and also these operations should be performed with least amount of space and time complexity possible.

Operations in Threaded Binary Tree

The average Time Complexity of the operations are:

- Insertion : **log(N)**
- Deletion : **log(N)**
- Searching : **log(N)**

Space complexity for all three operations are: O(1).

The time required for finding inorder predecessor or successor for a given node in Threaded Binary Tree is O(1) provided we are on that node.

Insert in Threaded Binary Tree

If we want to insert new node in threaded binary tree, then we can use insert operation. To insert any node in threaded binary tree, three cases might arise:

1. When new node is inserted in an empty tree.

2. When new node is inserted as left child of some node in the tree.

3. When new node is inserted as right child of some node in the tree.

Case 1

When new node is inserted in an empty threaded binary search tree, we set the new node's left and right pointers as null pointers. This step is same in both binary as well as threaded binary search tree.

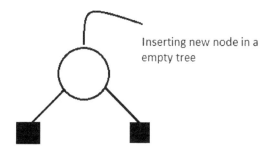

Inserting new node in a empty tree

Left and right pointers of new node are set to null

```
root = tmp;
tmp -> left = NULL;
tmp -> right = NULL;
```

Case 2

When new node is inserted in binary search tree as left child of some already existing node, then node we perform two operations in parent and two operations in child for example -

For Child

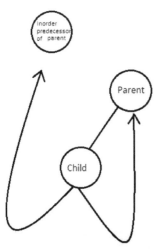

Setting left ptr of the child node to inorder predecessor of parent, and
right pointer of child to parent when new node is inserted as left child

For newly inserted child node, we set the new node's left child node point to left of
parent (that is Inorder predecessor of the parent node) and it's right child node
point to parent.

```
tmp -> left = par ->left;
tmp -> right = par;
```

For Parent

For parent of the child node inserted, we set it's lthread to true indicating left child
exist and also setting it's left child node as temp as child node is the new inorder
predecessor for the parent node and also it's the left child of the parent.

```
par -> lthread = true;
par -> left = temp;
```

Case 3

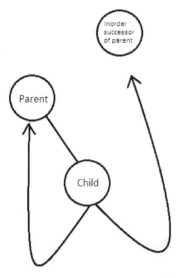

setting right ptr of child node to inorder successor of
parent node and left pointer of child to parent

When new node is inserted as right child of some node, we perform two operations
on the child and two operations on parent similar to what we have done in case 2 -

For Child

Let us say the new node inserted is child node and the node to which it's inserted is
parent node, then we can say that the parent of child inserted is now it's inorder
predecessor and the inorder successor of parent is now the inorder succesor for
the child node.

So, the left and right threads of the new node will be –

```
// tmp represent child node here

tmp -> left = par;
tmp -> right = par -> right;
```

For Parent

The right pointer of parent node now points to it's newly inserted node and setting up it's bool variable to true indicating there exists a right child.

```
// par represents parent node here
par -> rthread = true;
par -> right = tmp;
```

Complete pseudocode of insert operation is as follows:

```
// Insert a Node in Binary Threaded Tree
struct Node *insert(struct Node *root, int ikey)
{
    // Searching for a Node with given value
    Node *ptr = root;
    Node *par = NULL; // Parent of key to be inserted
    while (ptr != NULL)
    {
        // If key already exists, return
        if (ikey == (ptr->info))
        {
            printf("Duplicate Key !\n");
            return root;
        }

        par = ptr; // Update parent pointer

        // Moving on left subtree.
        if (ikey < ptr->info)
        {
            if (ptr -> lthread == false)
                ptr = ptr -> left;
            else
                break;
        }

        // Moving on right subtree.
        else
        {
            if (ptr->rthread == false)
                ptr = ptr -> right;
            else
```

```
                  break;
        }
    }

    // Create a new node
    Node *tmp = new Node;
    tmp -> info = ikey;
    tmp -> lthread = true;
    tmp -> rthread = true;

    if (par == NULL)
    {
        root = tmp;
        tmp -> left = NULL;
        tmp -> right = NULL;
    }
    else if (ikey < (par -> info))
    {
        tmp -> left = par -> left;
        tmp -> right = par;
        par -> lthread = false;
        par -> left = tmp;
    }
    else
    {
        tmp -> left = par;
        tmp -> right = par -> right;
        par -> rthread = false;
        par -> right = tmp;
    }

    return root;
}
```

Time and space complexity for insertion

- Time complexity - O(log N)
- Space complexity - O(1)

Search operation in Threaded Binary Tree

209

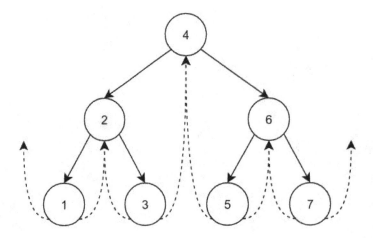

Search operation in threaded binary tree is pretty simple we just need to follow a simple algorithm that is shown below

```
If search key < root then
    Go to left thread
else
    Go to right thread
```

We need to keep repeating the above algorithm until we find the required node , if we are unable to locate the node and reach null we can return -1 indicating that element does not exist in the tree.

The pseudocode following the above approach is as follows:

```
struct Node *search( struct Node *root , int key ){

    Node *ptr = root ;

    while( ptr != nullptr ){

        if( ptr->info == key ){
            // indicating that the element is found then
```

210

```
            return ptr ;
        }else if( ptr->info < key ){
            // moving to inorder predecessor of the current node
            ptr = ptr->right ;
        }else{
            // moving to inorder successor of the current node
            ptr = ptr->left ;
        }


    }

    // if element is not found then we can return nullptr
indicating element not
    // found in the given binary search tree
    return nullptr ;


}
```

Time and space complexity for searching

- Time complexity: O(log N)
- Space complexity: O(1)

Delete operation in Threaded Binary Tree

If we want to delete some node from the given doubly threaded binary search tree, then we can use the delete operation but in the delete operation there can be three cases for a node in a doubly threaded binary tree:

- Case 1: leaf node needs to be deleted
- Case 2: node to be deleted has only 1 child left or right
- Case 3: node to be deleted has 2 children

Case 1 leaf node needs to be deleted

If we are deleting any node which is a leaf node, then it's parent's left or right thread need to be adjusted so if leaf node is left child of the parent node, then:

211

- after deletion left thread of the parent node is made to point to left thread of the child
- and parent's leftThread is set to false indicating parent is pointing to some inorder predecessor.

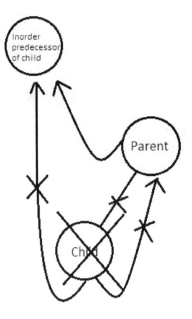

If the child node needs to be deleted is the left child then left pointer of the parent will now point to inorder predecessor of the child

```
parent -> lthread = true;
parent -> left = ptr -> left;
```

Similarly, if we are deleting the right child, then parent's right is made to point to right thread of child and rightThread is set to false.

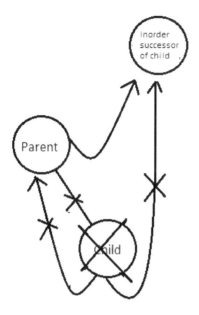

If node to be deleted is right child then right
pointer of parent will now point to inorder
successor of child node

```
par -> rthread = true;
par -> right = ptr -> right;
```

Pseudocode for case 1 of deletion:

```
struct Node* case1(struct Node* root, struct Node* par,
                   struct Node* ptr)
{
    // If Node to be deleted is root
    if (par == NULL)
        root = NULL;

    // If Node to be deleted is left
    // of its parent
    else if (ptr == par->left) {
```

```
        par->lthread = true;
        par->left = ptr->left;
    }
    else {
        par->rthread = true;
        par->right = ptr->right;
    }

    // Free memory and return new root
    free(ptr);
    return root;
}
```

Case 2: node to be deleted has only 1 child left or right

Before deleting such node first it's inorder predecessor and inorder successor is found out:

```
s = inSucc(ptr);
p = inPred(ptr);
```

then,

If Node to be deleted has left subtree, then after deletion right thread of its inorder predecessor should point to its inorder successor.

```
p->left = s;
```

If Node to be deleted has right subtree, then after deletion left thread of its inorder successor should point to its inorder predecessor .

```
s->left = p ;
```

Code for case 2

214

```
struct Node* case2(struct Node* root, struct Node* par,
                   struct Node* ptr)
{
    struct Node* child;

    // Initialize child Node to be deleted has
    // left child.
    if (ptr->lthread == false)
        child = ptr->left;

    // Node to be deleted has right child.
    else
        child = ptr->right;

    // Node to be deleted is root Node.
    if (par == NULL)
        root = child;

    // Node is left child of its parent.
    else if (ptr == par->left)
        par->left = child;
    else
        par->right = child;

    // Find successor and predecessor
    Node* s = inSucc(ptr);
    Node* p = inPred(ptr);

    // If ptr has left subtree.
    if (ptr->lthread == false)
        p->right = s;

    // If ptr has right subtree.
    else {
        if (ptr->rthread == false)
            s->left = p;
    }

    free(ptr);
    return root;
}
```

215

Case 3: node to be deleted has 2 children

We find inorder successor of Node to be deleted and then we copy the information of this inorder successor into current Node. After this inorder successor Node is deleted using either Case 1 or Case 2 explained above.

```
// Here 'par' is pointer to parent Node and 'ptr' is
// pointer to current Node.
struct Node* case3(struct Node* root, struct Node* par,
                   struct Node* ptr)
{
    // Find inorder successor and its parent.
    struct Node* parsucc = ptr;
    struct Node* succ = ptr->right;

    // Find leftmost child of successor
    while (succ->left != NULL) {
        parsucc = succ;
        succ = succ->left;
    }

    ptr->info = succ->info;

    if (succ->lthread == true && succ->rthread == true)
        root = case1(root, parsucc, succ);
    else
        root = case2(root, parsucc, succ);

    return root;
}
```

Average Time and space complexity for deletion

- Time complexity: **O(log N)**
- Space complexity: **O(1)**

Insight:

The key idea in understanding the operations is that how changing the structure of a Binary Tree impacts the 3 basic operations. Threaded Binary Tree is a variant of

216

Binary Tree as an example. In real problems, we may need to develop other variants and tune the 3 basic operations accordingly.

Convert Binary Tree to Threaded Binary Tree

We will focus on 2 different approaches on how to convert a normal binary tree into a threaded binary tree. We will convert our binary tree to single threaded binary tree with right pointers pointing to inorder successor (if it exists).

You may apply the same ideas to convert it to **Double Threaded Binary Tree**.

Approach 1: Naive Approach

We can do the inorder traversal of the tree and store it in a queue. Do another inorder traversal and wherever we find a node whose right child node reference is NULL, we will take the front element from the queue and make it the right of the current node.

This approach is easy to follow but the problem with this approach is it use extra memory and also, it is traversing the tree two times which makes approach 1 quite heavy on space and time.

Time Complexity : O(N)

Space Complexity : O(N)

Instead of following this approach we can do better , so let us have a look at approach 2.

Approach 2

In this approach, we will take a recursive approach. The Algorithmic steps are as follows:

1. Do the reverse inorder traversal which means visit right child first then parent followed by left child.
2. In each recursive call, pass the node which you have visited before visiting current node.

218

---

3. In each recursive call whenever you encounter a node whose right pointer is set to NULL and previous visited node is set to not NULL then, make the right pointer of node points to previously visited node and mark the value rightThread as true.

Whenever making a new recursive call to right subtree, do not change the previous visited node and when making a recursive call to left subtree, pass the actual previous visited node.

Remember that when our right pointer of the current node is pointing to it's children node, bool rightThread it set to true and if it is pointing to some of it's ancestor, then rightThread is set to false.

This approach is better than the previous approach as this uses less time and much less constant space.

Let us look at an example to see how we can use this algorithm to convert a binary tree to threaded binary tree.

Consider the following tree as an example:

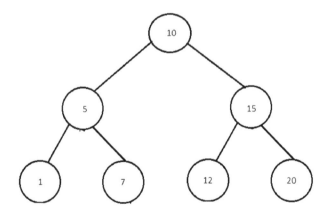

Step 1 :-

In the given tree, we will traverse the tree in reverse inorder traversal which means we will first visit the right subtree then root then followed by the left subtree.

Step 2 :-

As we will follow this algorithm recursively , so first we will visit the rightmost leaf node 20 , since there is no need which we have visited prior to this node we will make it's right pointer point to NULL and bool variable as false.

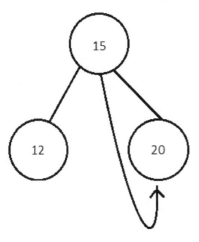

Step 3 :-

Now we will move to root which is node 15 in the given case and since we have already visited node 20 prior to node 15 so we will mark the right pointer of current node (15) to 20 and make bool but currently we are not on the leaf node so we will also make rightThread bool variable as true (indicating it's pointing to it's child node).

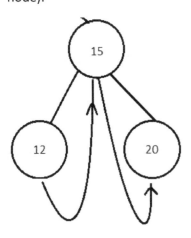

220

Step 4 :-

We will again repeat the step three on node 12 but this is a leaf node whose right pointer is pointing to it's ancestor so we will set rightThread bool variable as false.

Step 5 :-

We will just keep repeating the steps 2, 3 and 4 until whole tree is traversed just keeping one thing mind - whenever we make a new recursive call to right subtree, do not change the previous visited node and when we make a recursive call to left subtree then pass the actual previous visited node .

Step 6 :-

At the end we will have the whole binary tree converted to threaded binary tree.

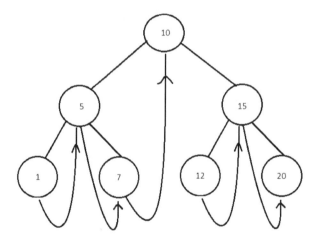

The time and space complexity required for the above conversion is:

- Time Complexity : O(N)
- Space Complexity : O(1) [Not considering the space consumed by recursive calls]

The Pseudocode of this approach is as follows:

```
class BSTtoThreadedBST {

    public :

    BSTtoThreadedBST(){

    }

    void convert(Node *root){
        inorder(root, nullptr);
    }

    void inorder(Node *root, Node *previous){

        if(root==nullptr){
            return;
        }else{
            inorder(root->right, previous);
            if(root->right==nullptr &&  previous!=nullptr){
                root->right = previous;
                root->rightThread=true;
            }
            inorder(root->left, root);
        }
    } ;

    void print(Node *root){
        //first go to most left node
        Node *current = leftMostNode(root);
        //now travel using right pointers
        while(current!=nullptr){
            cout<<" "<<current->data ;
            //check if node has a right thread
            if(current->rightThread)
                current = current->right;
            else
            // else go to left most node in the right subtree
                current = leftMostNode(current->right);
        }
        cout<<endl;
```

```
        }
    } ;
```

With this, you should have the complete idea.

Make sure to attempt to design a variant of our algorithm that will convert a Binary Tree to a Doubled Threaded Binary Tree.

Insight:

We explored how we can convert a simple Binary Tree to one of its variants, Single Threaded Binary Tree. This is an important path as for many problems, it is better to change the structure than to work on the original structure.

223

Binary Search Tree

Binary Search Tree is a variant of Binary Tree just like ***Threaded Binary Tree*** and ***Skewed Binary Tree***. It has a pattern between the parent node and child nodes that the value of left child node is less than the parent node and the value of right child node is greater than the parent node.

This data structure allows us to *maintain a sorted list of numbers in a tree data structure* in an efficient way.

It is called a *search tree* because it can be used to search for the presence of a number in **O(logN)** time in contrast to O(N) time for a simple Binary Tree or array list.

The properties that separate a binary search tree from a regular binary tree are:

- All nodes of left subtree are less than root node
- All nodes of right subtree are more than root node
- Each sub-tree in a BST is a BST

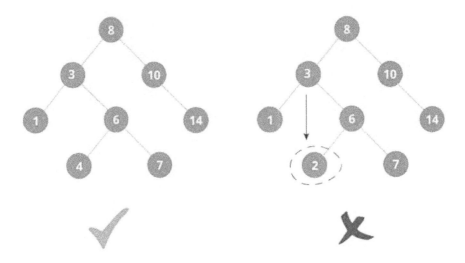

The binary tree on the right is **not** a binary search tree because the right subtree of the node "3" contains a value smaller than it.

224

A binary search tree node looks as follows:

```
BSTnode node
{
    int data;
    BSTnode left_node;
    BSTnode right_node;
}
```

It is the operations following the above restrictions that makes BST special.

There are three basic operations that you can perform on a binary search tree:

- Traversing/ searching (checking if a number is present)
- Inserting a number
- Deleting a number

1. Check if a number is present in Binary Search Tree

The algorithm to search a number in BST depends on the property of BST that each left subtree has values less than the root and each right subtree has values greater than the root.

If value is less than the root, we can say for sure that the value is not in the right subtree; we need to only search in the left subtree and if the value is above root, we can say for sure that the value is not in the left subtree; we need to only search in the right subtree.

Algorithm

```
If root==NULL
```

```
        return NULL;
    If number==root->data
        return root->data;
    If number<root->data
        return search(root->left)
    If number>root->data
        return search(root->right)
```

Let us try to visualize this with a diagram.

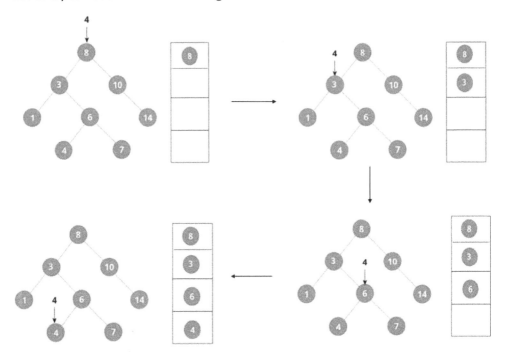

If the value is found, we return the value so that it gets propagated in each recursion step as show in the image below.

If you might have noticed , we have called return search(struct node*) four times. When we return either the new node or NULL, the value gets returned again and again until search(root) returns the final result.

226

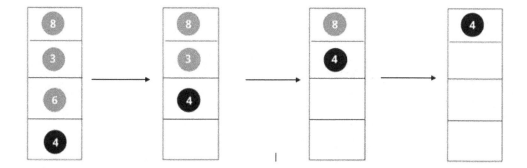

Following is the recursive implementation of search operation in BST:

```
// A utility function to search a given node
bool search(struct node* root, int key)
{
    // Base Cases: root is null or key is present at root
    if (root == NULL || root->key == key)
        return true;

    // Key is greater than root's key
    if (root->key < key)
        return search(root->right, key);

    // Key is smaller than root's key
    return search(root->left, key);
}
```

Can you implement the above function in an iterative way?

Try it on your own first.

Following is the iterative implementation of search operation in BST:

```
void searchKey(Node* &curr, int key, Node* &parent)
{
        while (curr != nullptr && curr->data != key)
        {
```

227

```
        // update parent node as current node
        parent = curr;

        // if given key is less than the current
        // node, go to left subtree
        // else go to right subtree
        if (key < curr->data)
                curr = curr->left;
        else
                curr = curr->right;

    }
}
```

2. Insert value in Binary Search Tree (BST)

Inserting a value in the correct position is similar to searching because we try to maintain the rule that left subtree is lesser than root and right subtree is larger than root.

We keep going to either right subtree or left subtree depending on the value and when we reach a point left or right subtree is null, we put the new node there.

Algorithm

```
If node == NULL
    return createNode(data)
if (data<node->data)
    node->left=insert(node->left,data);
else if (data > node->data)
    node->right = insert(node->right,data);
return node;
```

The algorithm is not as simple as it looks. Let us try to visualize how we add a number to an existing BST.

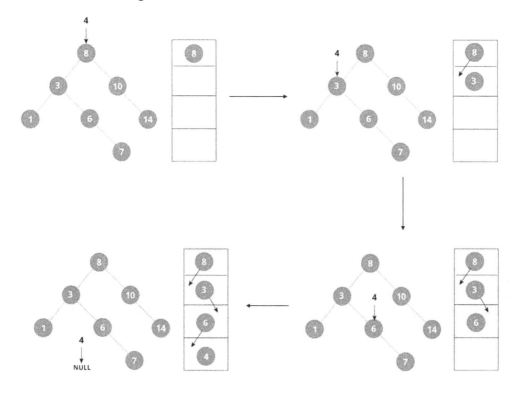

We have attached the node, but we still have to exit from the function without doing any damage to the rest of the tree. This is where the return node; at the end comes in handy. In the case of NULL, the newly created node is returned and attached to the parent node, otherwise the same node is returned without any change as we go up until we return to the root.

This makes sure that as we move back up the tree, the other node connections are not changed.

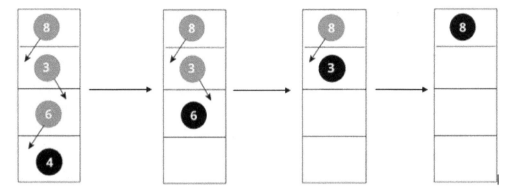

Implementation of above pseudocode

```c
// C program to demonstrate insert operation in binary search
tree
#include<stdio.h>
#include<stdlib.h>

struct node
{
    int key;
    struct node *left, *right;
};

// A utility function to create a new BST node
struct node *newNode(int item)
{
    struct node *temp = (struct node *)malloc(sizeof(struct
node));
    temp->key = item;
    temp->left = temp->right = NULL;
    return temp;
}

/* A utility function to insert a new node with
   given key in BST
*/
struct node* insert(struct node* node, int key)
{
    struct node *newNode(int);
    /* If the tree is empty, return a new node */
    if (node == NULL) return newNode(key);
```

```
    /* Otherwise, recur down the tree */
    if (key < node->key)
        node->left  = insert(node->left, key);
    else if (key > node->key)
        node->right = insert(node->right, key);

    /* return the (unchanged) node pointer */
    return node;
}

// Driver Program to test above functions
int main()
{
    struct node* insert(struct node* , int);
    struct node *root = NULL;
    root = insert(root, 8);
    insert(root, 3);
    insert(root, 10);
    insert(root, 1);
    insert(root, 6);
    insert(root, 4);
    insert(root, 7);
    insert(root, 5);
    insert(root, 10);
    insert(root, 9);
    insert(root, 13);
    insert(root, 11);
    insert(root, 14);
    insert(root, 12);
    insert(root, 2);
    return 0;
}
```

Example

Illustration to insert 2 in above tree:

Start from root which in this case is 8.

231

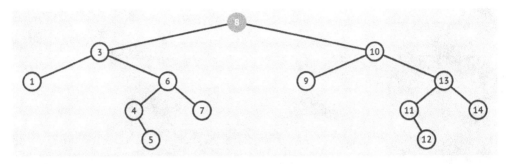

Now Check if the value that is 2 is less than root that is 8 then go to left of the 8.

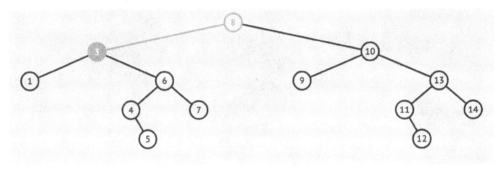

Now current node is 3 compare the value that is 2 with current node if the value is less than 3 go to left side of 3.

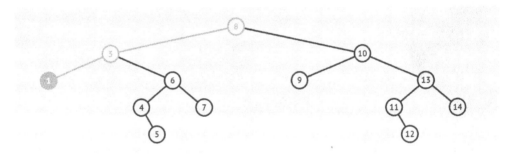

Now current node is 1 compare the value that is 2 with current node if the value is less than 1 go to left side of 1 else go to the right.

Now if the node is equal to null therefore create new node and insert it.

232

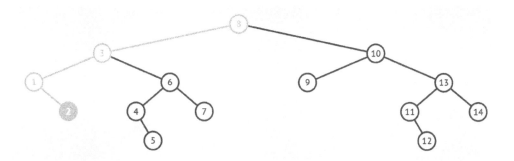

3. Deletion in a binary search tree

We must delete a node from a binary search tree in such a way, that the property of binary search tree does not violate. There are three situations of deleting a node from binary search tree:

- The node to be deleted is a leaf node
- The node to be deleted has only one child
- The node to be deleted has two children

1. The node to be deleted is a leaf node

In this case we will simply replace the leaf node with the NULL and allocated space will be freed. Example:

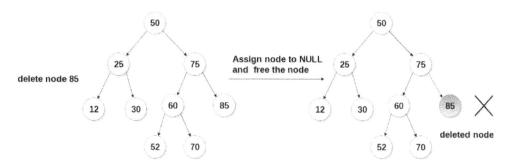

In the above figure, we are deleting the node 85, since the node is a leaf node, therefore the node will be replaced with NULL and allocated space will be freed.

233

2. The node to be deleted has only one child

In this case, replace the node with its child and delete the child node, which now contains the values to be deleted. Simply replace it with the NULL and free the allocated space.

Example:

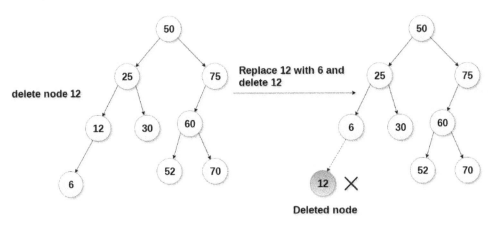

In the above figure, the node 12 is to be deleted. It has only one child. The node will be replaced with its child node and the replaced node 12 (which is now leaf node) will simply be deleted.

3. The node to be deleted has two children

The node which is to be deleted, is replaced with its in-order successor or predecessor recursively until the node value (to be deleted) is placed on the leaf of the tree. After the procedure replace the node with NULL and free the allocated space.

Example:

234

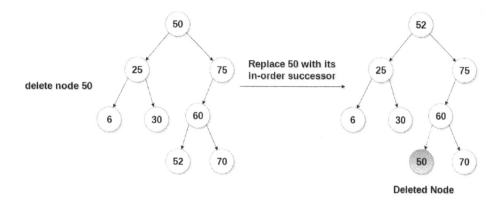

delete node 50

Replace 50 with its
in-order successor

Deleted Node

In the above figure, the node 50 is to be deleted which is the root node of the tree. The in-order traversal of the tree given below.

6, 25, 30, 50, 52, 60, 70, 75.

Replace 50 with its in-order successor 52. Now, 50 will be moved to the leaf of the tree, which will simply be deleted.

Code for delete in a BST

```cpp
// A utility function to delete node from a BST
void deleteNode(Node*& root, int key)
{
        // pointer to store parent node of current node
        Node* parent = nullptr;
        // start with root node
        Node* curr = root;
        // search key in BST and set its parent pointer
        searchKey(curr, key, parent);
        // return if key is not found in the tree
        if (curr == nullptr)
                return;

        // Case 1: node to be deleted has no children
        // that is it is a leaf node
        if (curr->left == nullptr && curr->right == nullptr)
        {
                // if node to be deleted is not a root
```

235

```
                 // node, then set its
                 // parent left/right child to null
                 if (curr != root)
                 {
            if (parent->left == curr)
                             parent->left = nullptr;
                     else
                             parent->right = nullptr;
                 }
                 // if tree has only root node, delete it
                 // and set root to null
                 else
                         root = nullptr;
                 // deallocate the memory
                 free(curr);         // or delete curr;
        }

        // Case 2: node to be deleted has two children
        else if (curr->left && curr->right)
        {
                 // find its in-order successor node
                 Node* successor  = minimumKey(curr->right);
                 // store successor value
                 int val = successor->data;
                 // recursively delete the successor.
                 // Note that the successor
                 // will have at-most one child (right child)
                 deleteNode(root, successor->data);
                 // Copy the value of successor to current node
                 curr->data = val;
        }
        // Case 3: node to be deleted has only one child
        else
        {
                 Node* child = (curr->left)? curr->left: curr-
>right;
                 // if node to be deleted is not a root
                 // node, then set its parent to its child
                 if (curr != root)
                 {
                         if (curr == parent->left)
                                 parent->left = child;
                         else
                                 parent->right = child;
                 }
```

```
          // if node to be deleted is root node,
          // then set the root to child
          else
                  root = child;
          // deallocate the memory
          free(curr);
      }
}
```

Complexity

Searching

- Worst case time complexity :**O(n)**
- Average case time complexity :**O(h)**, where h is height of BST.

where N is the number of elements in the Binary Search Tree

h = log N for a balanced binary search tree. Hence, range of h is from log N to N.

Insertion

- Worst case time complexity: O(n)
- Average case time complexity: O(h)

Deletion

- Worst case complexity: O(n)
- Average case time complexity: O(h)

Advantages

We can always keep the cost of insert(), delete(), lookup() to **O(logN)** where N is the number of nodes in the tree - so the benefit really is that lookups can be done in logarithmic time which matters a lot when N is large.

237

To give you an idea, if N = 1,048,576 (that is more than 1M), the **logN** is just 20. Hence, in a Balanced Binary Search Tree with 1M element, we can search an element just by comparing 20 elements.

We can have ordering of keys stored in the tree. Any time we need to traverse the increasing (or decreasing) order of keys, we just need to do the in-order (and reverse in-order) traversal on the tree.

We can implement order statistics with binary search tree - N^{th} smallest, N^{th} largest element. This is because it is possible to look at the data structure as a sorted array.

We can also do range queries-find keys between N and M (N<=M).

BST can also be used in the design of memory allocators to speed up the search of free blocks (chunks of memory) and to implement best fit algorithms where we are interested in finding the smallest free chunk with size greater than or equal to size specified in an allocation request.

Applications

A Self-Balancing Binary Search Tree is used to maintain sorted stream of data. For example, suppose we are getting online orders placed and we want to maintain the live data (in RAM) in sorted order of prices.

For example, suppose we wish to know number of items purchased at cost below a given cost at any moment. Or we wish to know number of items purchased at higher cost than given cost.

A Self-Balancing Binary Search Tree is used to implement doubly ended priority queue. With a Binary Heap, we can either implement a priority queue with support of exctractMin() or with extractMax(). If we wish to support of extractMin() or with extractMax(). If we wish to support both the operations, we use a Self-Balancing Binary Search Tree to do both in O(logN).

There are many more algorithm problems where a Self-Balancing BST is the best suited data structure, like count smaller on right, Smallest Greater on Right Side and many more.

Insight:

Binary Tree has a structure and if we are able to distribute the data according to a certain pattern, then we can make use of the structure to gain advantage. This is the fundamental idea of Binary Search Tree.

As we move forward in this book, you will see another variant based on this idea: Binary Space Partitioning Tree.

Converting a Sorted Array to Binary Tree

Sorted array is converted to Binary Search Tree for faster search operations and querying. We will learn to convert any sorted array to binary search tree.

For converting a sorted array to binary tree, we will need an array which is unsorted and sort it first. Then, we will make the middle element of the array as the root of the tree and make the left children as the left subset of the array, similarly the right part will be the right subset of the array.

Approach:

Let say we have an array A:

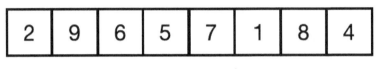

Unsorted Array

We will sort this array.

For this, we can use a standard function available in your Programming Language of choice. For example, we cans sort using the inbuilt sort() function in standard template library (STL) in C++ in ascending order. First, we will take an array with name "arr1" and fill the values {2,9,6,5,7,1,8,4} and sort it.

Code:

```cpp
#include <bits/stdc++.h>
using namespace std;

int main()
{
    vector<int> arr;
    int arr1[8] = {2,9,6,5,7,1,8,4};
    for(auto x:arr1) arr.push_back(x);
    sort(arr.begin(),arr.end());
    //Further code...
```

240

```
}
```

After sorting the array becomes,

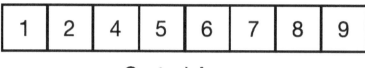

Sorted Array

As the array is now sorted, we can implement the tree data structure to store the values of the array elements.

Implementation of tree:

For the implementation of tree, we need a Node class which defines a tree node to store data and pointers to left and right subtree.

So, we can create a Node class by the following syntax:

```
class Node {
    public:
        int data;
        Node* left;
        Node* right;
}
```

After the creation of Node class, we can implement the tree functions which are inserting nodes and traversing them.

Firstly, we will need function to make an empty tree node in the memory,

```
Node* newNode(int data)
{
    // This line allocates the memory of a Node in the storage.
    Node* newnode = new Node();
```

241

```
    //This line sets the data into the node
    newnode->data = data;
    //This line sets the left and right pointers to NULL
    newnode->right = NULL;
    newnode->left = NULL;
    return newnode;
}
```

Then, we will create a function which takes in an array or vector which is sorted as its input and creates a balanced binary search tree.

For implementation, we will take vector as it's input and then find the mid element of the list, we will take this element as root and find the mid elements of left and right subtree recursively to create a balanced tree.

Algorithm (recursive version):

1. Take a sorted array.

2. Find the mid element of the array and insert into the tree.

3. Find the mid element of left and right tree and insert into the array.

4. Repeat until no element is left.

Implementation of the above algorithm (recursive version) :

Step 1: Take a sorted array into the function.

```
Node* sortedArrayToBST(vector<int>& arr,
                       int start, int end)
{
```

Step 2: Find the mid element of the array and insert into the tree.

```
//If starting index goes beyond end index then return NULL
    if (start > end)
        return NULL;

    //Compute the middle index and make it as root.
    int mid = (start + end)/2;
    Node *root = newNode(arr[mid]);
```

Step 3 & 4: Find the mid element of left and right tree and insert into the array.
Repeat until no element is left.

```
//Recursively create left and right subtrees.
    root->left = sortedArrayToBST(arr, start, mid - 1);
    root->right = sortedArrayToBST(arr, mid + 1, end);

    //Return the root element which is the middle element of the
list
    return root;
}
```

Conversion from sorted array to BST takes N steps as the function has to go over
every element once, hence the time complexity is O(N).

So, the sorted array becomes,

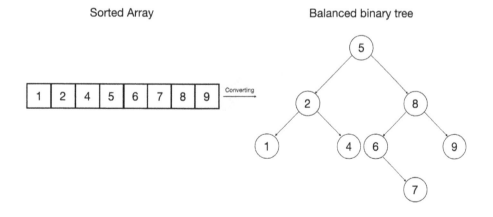

243

Algorithm (iterative version):

1. Take a sorted array and take a stack.

2. Each tuple keeps track of the child's parent and the side of the parent that the child will become.

3. We only push child tuples to the stack after their parents are created, the process will create the children until we reach the base case, whereby that branch has exhausted its corresponding chunk of the original elements.

Implementation of the above algorithm (iterative version) :

Step 1: First we will create a struct T, with low_idx, high_idx and node. This can be a class depending on the Programming Language you are using. The idea remains the same.

```
struct T {
    int low_idx;
    int high_idx;
    Node node;
    Tree(int low, int high, Node _node) {
        low_idx = low
        high_idx = high
        node = _node
    }
}
```

Step 2: Then we will create a function sortedArrayToBST.

```
Node sortedArrayToBST(int A[], int n) {
```

Step 3: Return if the length of array is 0

```
if (n == 0)
```

244

```
     return NULL;
```

Step 4: Create stack and push the node with middle element of array.

```
stack<int> S;
Node root = new Node(A[(n - 1)/2])
T tree = new T(0, n - 1, root)
S.push(tree);
while (!S.empty()) {
```

Step 5: Pop the top node and assign the left and right child to it.

```
T tmp = S.top();
S.pop();
int mid = tmp.low_idx + (tmp.high_idx - tmp.low_idx) / 2;
```

Step 6: If the lower index of tmp element is less than mid we will pick middle element and push that into the tree.

```
if (tmp.low_idx < mid) {
      Node node = new Node(A[tmp.low_idx +
            (mid - 1 - tmp.low_idx) / 2]);
      tmp.node.left_idx = node;
      tree = new T(tmp.low_idx, mid - 1, node);
      S.push(tree);
}
```

Step 7: If the higher index of tmp element is greater than the mid we will pick middle element of high_idx and mid then push that into the tree.

```
if (mid < tmp.high_idx) {
      Node node = new Node(A[mid + 1 + (tmp.high_idx - mid -
1)/2]);
```

245

```
            tmp.node.right_idx = node;
            tree = new T(mid + 1, tmp.high_idx, node);
            S.push(tree);
    }
}
return root;
}
```

Conversion from sorted array to BST takes n steps as the function has to go over every element once, hence the time complexity is O(n)

So, the sorted array becomes,

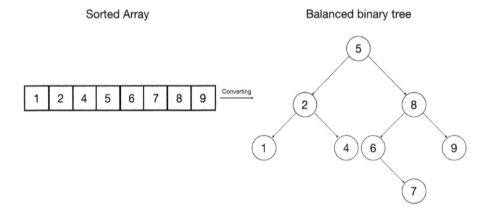

Sorted Array   Balanced binary tree

Now, you can implement various traversals such as inorder, preorder and postorder. For this example we will demonstrate preorder traversal method.

In the preorder traversal method, first the root is traversed then the left subtree and then the right subtree.

We will create a function for this purpose,

```
void preOrder(Node* root){
    if (!root) return;
    cout << root->data << " ";
    preOrder(root->left);
```

246

```
    preOrder(root->right);
}
```

Time Complexity: O(N)

Hence, the complete function to convert an array to a Binary Search Tree is as follows:

```
Node* sortedArrayToBST(vector<int>& arr,
                       int start, int end)
{
    //If starting index goes beyond end index then return NULL
    if (start > end)
        return NULL;

    //Compute the middle index and make it as root.
    int mid = (start + end)/2;
    Node *root = newNode(arr[mid]);

    //Recursively create left and right subtrees.
    root->left = sortedArrayToBST(arr, start, mid - 1);
    root->right = sortedArrayToBST(arr, mid + 1, end);

    //Return the root element which is the middle
    //element of the list
    return root;
}
```


With this, you must have the complete idea.

Insight:

This is important as you should realize that we are converting one data structure (array) to another data structure (Binary Search Tree) and are preserving the properties of the original data structure (that is: sorted order).

247

Following this, you will realize that at the end, it is the restrictions that define a data structure, and all other properties are *interchangeable*.

Minimum number of swaps to convert a binary tree to binary search tree

We understand that a Binary Tree is an unrestricted version of Binary Search Tree. It is the order of elements that differentiate both variants. Swapping is a fundamental operation where two elements are interchanged.

The problem is to find the minimum number of swaps to convert a Binary Tree to a Binary Search Tree.

Question: What is the maximum number of swaps required? The exact number depends on the Binary Tree we are working with.

By the property of Binary Search Tree, we know that by doing Inorder Traversal, we get a sorted list of elements.

The **Idea** is do the inorder traversal of Binary Tree and store it in an array. Then, find the minimum number of swaps require to sort an array which is the output we want.

How to do Inorder Traversal of Binary Tree?

Unlike linear data structures (Array, Linked List, Queue, Stack) which have only one logical way to traverse them, trees can be traversed in different ways. One of the way is **Inorder Traversal**.

Algorithm Inorder (recursive):

  1. Traverse the left subtree that is call Inorder(left-subtree)

  2. Visit the root.

  3. Traverse the right subtree that is call Inorder(right-subtree)

How to find the Minimum Number of Swaps to form the sorted array?

249

Given an array of N distinct elements, find the minimum number of swaps required to sort the array.

Examples:

Input: {4,2,5,1,3}

Output: 2

Explanation:

Swap index 0 with 3 and 2 with 4 to form the sorted array {1, 2, 3, 4, 5}.

This can be easily done by visualizing the problem as a graph. We will have N nodes and an edge directed from node i to node j if the element at i^{th} index must be present at j^{th} index in the sorted array.

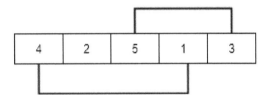

The graph will now contain many non-intersecting cycles. Now a cycle with 2 nodes will only require 1 swap to reach the correct ordering.

Hence,

summation of i = 1 to k: **ans = Σ i = (cycle_size − 1)**

where k is the number of cycles

Approach:

Create an array of pairs where first element is an array element and second element is position of first element.

Sort the array by array element values to get right position of every element as second element of pair.

To keep track of visited elements, initialize all elements as not visited or false.

250

Traverse array elements and find out the number of nodes in this cycle and add in ans and Update answer by adding current cycle.

Implementation of above approach.

```cpp
// Function returns the minimum number of swaps
// required to sort the array
int minSwaps(int arr[], int n)
{
    // Create an array of pairs where first
    // element is array element and second element
    // is position of first element
    pair<int, int> arrPos[n];
    for (int i = 0; i < n; i++)
    {
        arrPos[i].first = arr[i];
        arrPos[i].second = i;
    }

    // Sort the array-by-array element values to
    // get right position of every element as second
    // element of pair.
    sort(arrPos, arrPos + n);

    // To keep track of visited elements. Initialize
    // all elements as not visited or false.
    vector<bool> vis(n, false);

    // Initialize result
    int ans = 0;

    // Traverse array elements
    for (int i = 0; i < n; i++)
    {
        // already swapped and corrected or
        // already present at correct pos
        if (vis[i] || arrPos[i].second == i)
            continue;

        // find out the number of  node in
        // this cycle and add in ans
        int cycle_size = 0;
```

```
            int j = i;
            while (!vis[j])
            {
                vis[j] = true;
                j = arrPos[j].second;
                cycle_size++;
            }

            // Update answer by adding current cycle.
            if (cycle_size > 0)
            {
                ans += (cycle_size - 1);
            }
        }

    return ans;
}
```

Now by combing above two methods, we will get the minimum number of swaps to convert the binary tree into binary search tree

Approach:

Do the Inorder Traversal of the binary tree and store the elements of tree in an array.

Then find the minimum number of swaps require to make the array sorted which is made from above process and store it in result and give as output.

Time Complexity: **O(N logN)**

This is because minimum number of swaps is the minimum number of steps to sort an array. This is O(N logN).

Space Complexity: **O(N)**

This is because we need to store the inorder traversal of the original Binary Tree to find the minimum number of swaps.

Insights:

In the previous problem (converting a sorted array to Binary Search Tree), we understood that different Data Structures are the same with different restrictions.

Our current problem brings up a key point that this interchange between different Data Structures come *at a cost*.

Find minimum or maximum element in Binary Search Tree

The problem statement is that we are given a Binary Search Tree and we need to find the minimum or maximum element efficiently.

As we know the Property of Binary search tree. This quite simple

Approach for finding minimum element:

- Traverse the node from root to left recursively until left is NULL.
- The node whose left is NULL is the node with minimum value.

Approach for finding maximum element:

- Traverse the node from root to right recursively until right is NULL.
- The node whose right is NULL is the node with maximum value.

Implementation of the above approaches:

This is the implementation to find the minimum element in a Binary Search Tree:

```
/* Given a non-empty binary search tree,
return the minimum data value found in that
tree. Note that the entire tree does not need
to be searched. */
int minValue(struct node* node)
{
    struct node* current = node;

    /* loop down to find the leftmost leaf */
    while (current->left != NULL)
    {
        current = current->left;
    }
```

254

```
        return(current->key);
}
```

This is the implementation to find the maximum element in a Binary Search Tree:

```
/* Given a non-empty binary search tree,
return the maximum data value found in that
tree. Note that the entire tree does not need
to be searched. */
int maxValue(struct node* node)
{
    struct node* current = node;

    /* loop down to find the leftmost leaf */
    while (current->right != NULL)
    {
        current = current->right;
    }
    return(current->key);
}
```

Explanation:

For Finding Minimum value in Binary search tree.

start from root that is 8.

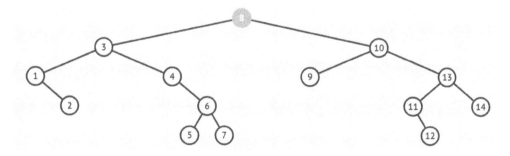

As left of root is not null go to left of root that is 3.

255

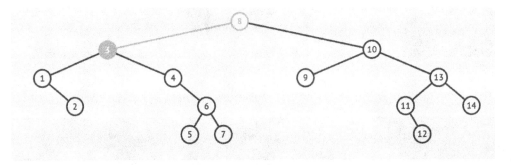

As left of 3 is not null go to left of 3 that is 1.

Now as the left of 1 is null therefore 1 is the minimum element

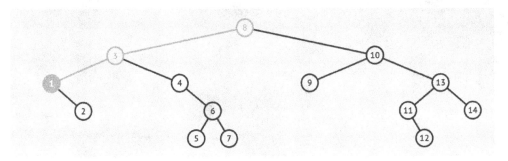

For Finding Maximum value in Binary search tree.

start from root that is 8.

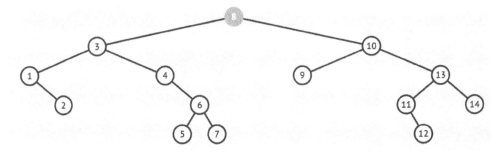

As right of root is not null go to right of root that is 10.

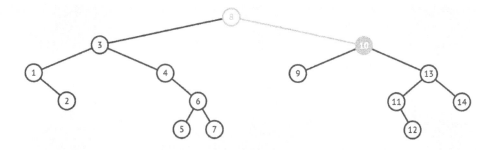

As right of 10 is not null go to right of root that is 13.

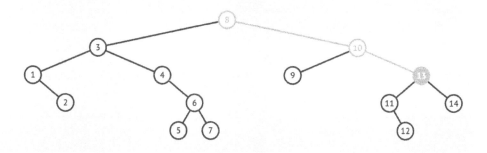

As right of 13 is not null go to right of root that is 14.

Now as the right of 14 is null therefore 14 is the maximum element.

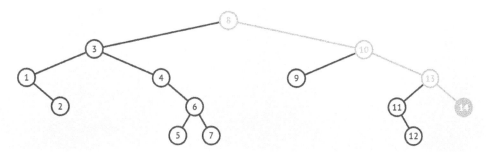

Time Complexity:

- O(N) Worst case happens for left skewed trees in finding the minimum value.
- O(N) Worst case happens for right skewed trees in finding the maximum value.
- O(1) Best case happens for left skewed trees in finding the maximum value.
- O(1) Best case happens for right skewed trees in finding the minimum value.
- In the balanced Binary Search tree, the time complexity is O(log N)

N is the number of elements in a Binary Search tree

257

Space complexity: O(1) as we need not store any information while finding the minimum or maximum element.

Insight:

This problem illustrates the power of Binary Search Tree.

We are able to find the minimum element in O(logN) time instead of O(N) time because the restriction in the structure of a Binary Search Tree has already done the extra work (O(N) – O(logN)) in other previous operations which we do not observe.

Hence, restrictions in a Data Structure make it suitable for specific problems.

Convert Binary Search Tree to Balanced Binary Search Tree

We will explore an algorithm to convert a Binary Search Tree (BST) into a Balanced Binary Search Tree. In a balanced BST, the height of the tree is log N where N is the number of elements in the tree.

In the worst case of an unbalanced BST, the height of the tree can be up to N which makes it *same as a linked list*. The height depends upon the order of insertion of elements while some other trees like AVL tree has routines to keep their tree balanced which is not present in a normal Binary Search Tree. It is important to keep a BST balanced, as it will give best performance for tasks it is built for like:

- searching elements in O(log N)

The conversion to a Balanced Binary Search Tree takes O(N) time complexity

Example:

Input of an unbalanced Binary Search Tree:

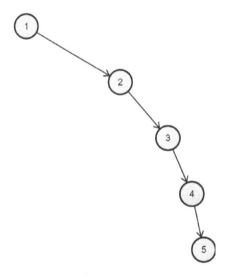

Output of the same tree but as a balanced Binary Search Tree:

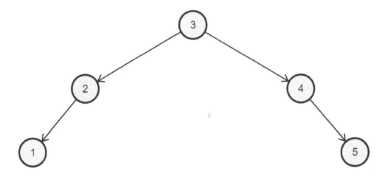

As we know the property of binary search tree, inorder traversal of binary search tree gives element in sorted order which are stored in binary search tree and then we can form the balanced binary search from the sorted array.

Algorithm:

- Traverse given BST in inorder and store result in an array. This step takes O(n) time. Note that this array would be sorted as inorder traversal of BST always produces sorted sequence.
- Get the Middle of the array and make it root.
- Recursively do same for left half and right half.
- Get the middle of left half and make it left child of the root created in step 1.
- Get the middle of right half and make it right child of the root created in step

Implementation

Following is the implementation of the above algorithm

```
/* This function traverse the skewed binary tree and
   stores its nodes pointers in vector nodes[] */
void storeBSTNodes(struct node* root, vector<struct node*>
&nodes)
{
    // Base case
    if (root==NULL)
        return;
```

260

```
    // Store nodes in Inorder (which is sorted
    // order for BST)
    storeBSTNodes(root->left, nodes);
    nodes.push_back(root);
    storeBSTNodes(root->right, nodes);
}

/* Recursive function to construct binary tree */
struct node* buildTreeUtil(vector<struct node*> &nodes, int
start,
                      int end)
{
    // base case
    if (start > end)
        return NULL;

    /* Get the middle element and make it root */
    int mid = (start + end)/2;
    struct node *root = nodes[mid];

    /* Using index in Inorder traversal, construct
       left and right subtress */
    root->left  = buildTreeUtil(nodes, start, mid-1);
    root->right = buildTreeUtil(nodes, mid+1, end);

    return root;
}

// This functions converts an unbalanced BST to
// a balanced BST
struct node* buildTree(struct node* root)
{
    // Store nodes of given BST in sorted order
    vector<struct node*> nodes;
    storeBSTNodes(root, nodes);

    // Constucts BST from nodes[]
    int n = nodes.size();
    return buildTreeUtil(nodes, 0, n-1);
}
```

Explanation:

First of all, we will do inorder traversal and store the elements in an array.

First go to the left of the root but it is null therefore go to the root of the tree and store it in an array.

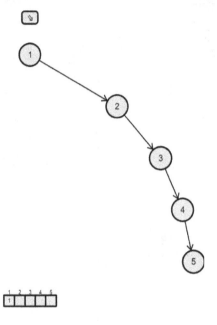

Then go to the right of the root go to the 2.left check if left child of the 2 is null the store 2 in the array.

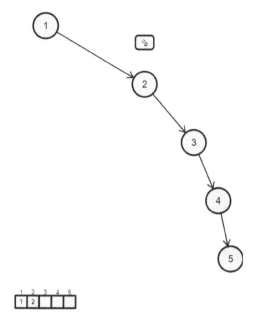

Then go to the right of the 2 and check if the left child of 3 is null the store the 3 in array.

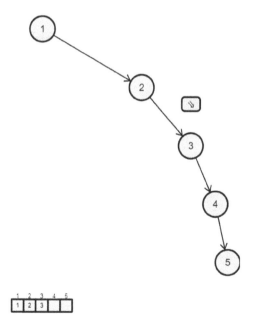

Then go to the right of 3 and check if the left child of 4 is null then store 5 in the array

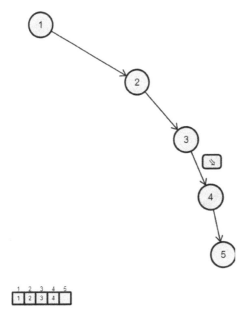

Then go to the right of 4 and check if the left child of 5 is null then store 5 in array. Now check if the right child of 5 is null then return the array.

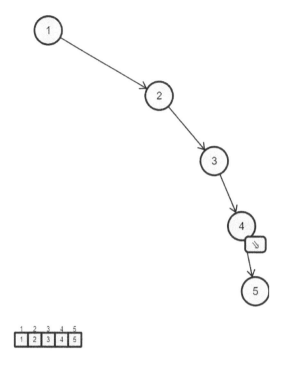

1	2	3	4	5
1	2	3	4	5

Now we will build the balanced binary search tree from the sorted array we obtained through the above process.

First of all, find the middle of the array that is 3 and store it as root of the new tree.

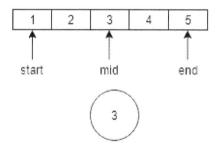

Then go to the left of the 3 and build the left subtree for that find again the middle of the left sub array of 3 that is 2 and store as the left child of 3.

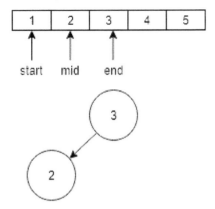

Then go the left sub array of the 2 and again find the middle of the array and store it as the left child of 2.

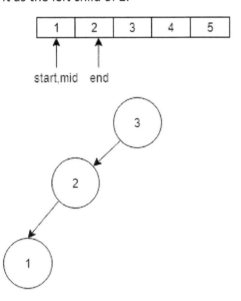

Now start > end therefore go to root of the tree that is 3.

Now as we have constructed left sub tree in similar way now, we will construct right sub tree go to the right sub array and again find the middle of the array that is 4 and store it as the right child of 3.

266

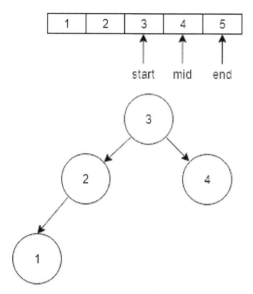

Now go the right sub array of 4 and again find the middle that is 5 and store it as the right child of the 4.

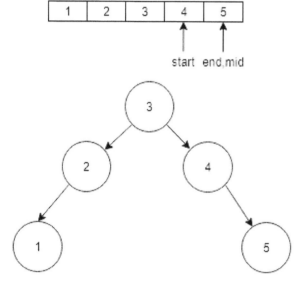

Now start>end return to root that is 3 of the tree. Now our Balanced Binary Search Tree is ready.

Time Complexity:

267

The Inorder Traversal of Binary search tree is in O(N) time complexity.

To form Balanced Binary tree from Sorted array, it takes O(N) time to complete.

Following is the recurrence relation for buildTreeUtil():

```
T(n) = 2T(n/2) + C
T(n) -->  Time taken for an array of size n
C    -->  Constant
(Finding middle of array
linking root to left and right subtrees take constant time)
```

Hence, the overall time complexity is **O(N)**.

The space complexity is **O(N)** as we need to store the elements in an array as sorted order.

Insight:

This is a key step as Binary Search Tree reaches its full potential only if it is balanced. To make it reach this, extra work is needed if this was not in consideration initially.

As we will see beyond, if we consider this initially, no extra load is necessary, and this leads to *"Self-Balancing Binary Tree"*

268

Find kth smallest element in Binary Search Tree

In previous problems, we have found the minimum and maximum element in a Binary Search Tree. In this problem, we need to find the kth smallest element in a Binary Search Tree. This does not seem to be simple compared to our previous problem.

Given root of the tree and k as input, output Kth smallest element.

For example, in below given tree, for k=3 we will get 5.

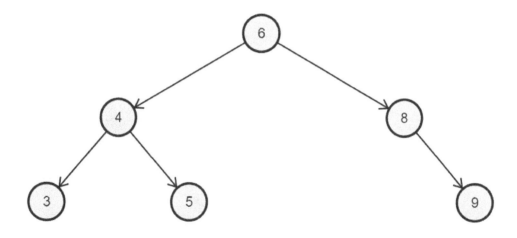

The idea simple do inorder traversal and store it an array. We know by the property of the binary search tree, inorder traversal gives element of a binary search tree in sorted form.

We will explore two approaches:

- Using inorder traversal (**O(N)**)
- Efficient approach (**O(log N)**)

Algorithm 1: Using inorder traversal O(N)

Do the Inorder traversal of the Binary search tree and store the elements in a vector in sequence.

Then from sorted vector made from above process return the kth element and it is the output we need.

Below is the Implementation of the above algorithm.

```cpp
/* This function traverse the skewed binary tree and
   stores its nodes pointers in vector nodes[] */
void storeBSTNodes(struct node* root, vector<struct node*>
&nodes)
{
    // Base case
    if (root==NULL)
        return;

    // Store nodes in Inorder (which is sorted
    // order for BST)
    storeBSTNodes(root->left, nodes);
    nodes.push_back(root);
    storeBSTNodes(root->right, nodes);
}

/* Recursive function to construct binary tree */


// This function find Kth Minimum Element in BST
int findKthMinimumElement(struct node* root,int k)
{
    // Store nodes of given BST in sorted order
    vector<struct node*> nodes;
    storeBSTNodes(root, nodes);

    return nodes[k-1]->key;
}
```

Explanation:

First of all, we go to the left most element of the tree and store it in a vector.

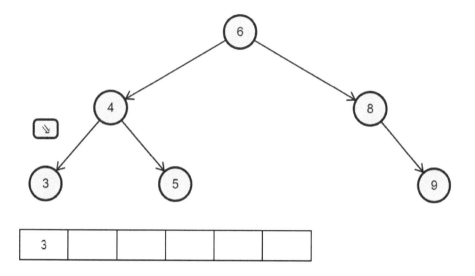

Then return back to parent element and store it in an array.

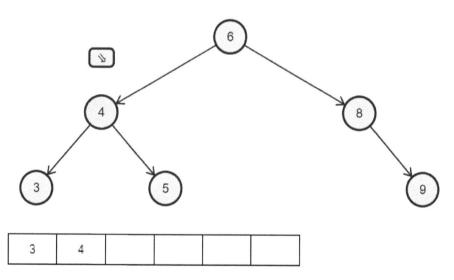

Then go to the right of present node and check it left child is present of right child of the present node then store it in an array and store it in vector.

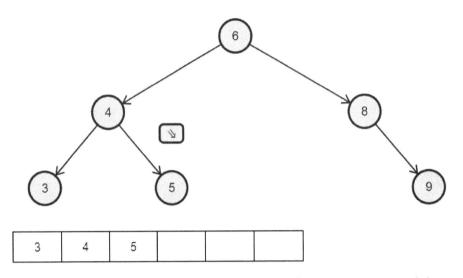

Then check the right children if it is not existing, then go to parent and then again return to parent of parent because it is visited and store it in vector.

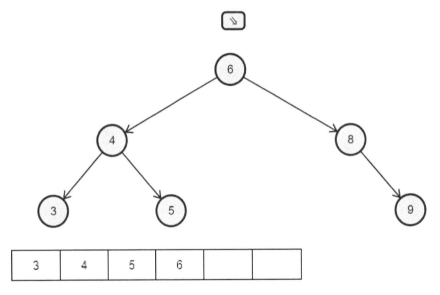

Then go to the right child of present node and check if left child does not exist the store the present node in vector.

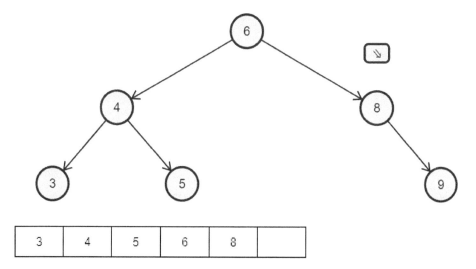

The right child of the present node and check if left child exist then go there otherwise store the present element in the vector.

Then check it right child exist then go there if not then, go to the root and now all the nodes are visited therefore return to the main function.

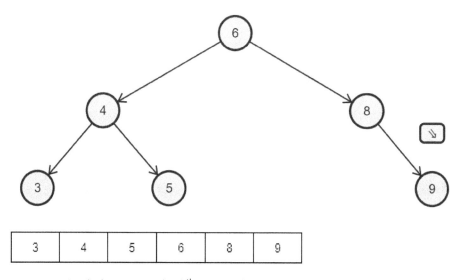

Now required element is the kth one in the array therefore return it and it is required output.

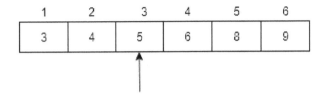

Time Complexity:

Inorder Traversal of Binary search Tree takes O(N) time and fetching the Kth element from vector requires O(1) time.

Therefore, all over time complexity of this algorithm is **O(N)**.

Efficient Approach O(log N)

The idea to maintain the rank of each node.

We will count the number of nodes in the left subtree of each node so this will give the rank of the node. It will help us to find the element in O(H) time where H is the height of the tree (H = logN for Balanced Binary Search Tree).

Algorithm:

```
start:
if K = root.leftElement + 1
    root node is the K th node.
    goto stop
else if K > root.leftElements
    K = K - (root.leftElements + 1)
    root = root.right
    goto start
else
    root = root.left
    goto start
```

274

Implementation of above algorithm in C++:

```cpp
int findKthMinimumElement(node *root, int k)
{
    int ret = -1;

    if( root )
    {
        /* A crawling pointer */
        node *pTraverse = root;

        /* Go to k-th smallest */
        while(pTraverse)
        {
            if( (pTraverse->lCount + 1) == k )
            {
                ret = pTraverse->data;
                break;
            }
            else if( k > pTraverse->lCount )
            {
                /*  There are less nodes on left subtree
                    Go to right subtree */
                k = k - (pTraverse->lCount + 1);
                pTraverse = pTraverse->right;
            }
            else
            {
                /* The node is on left subtree */
                pTraverse = pTraverse->left;
            }
        }
    }

    return ret;
}
```

275

Explanation:

Start with the root compare the lcount with k if k is equal to lcount then break if k<lcount then go the left otherwise go right. Subtract lCount+1 from k

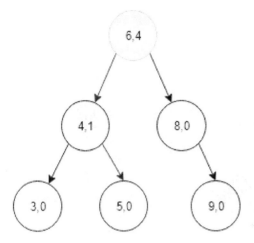

In our example, k is smaller then, lcount therefore we come to the left child now again compare lcount of the current node and k. Subtract lCount + 1 from k

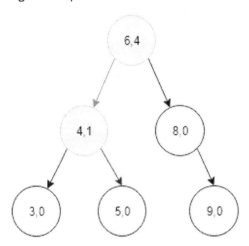

As we can see than lcount of the current node is less than k therefore, we go right child now.

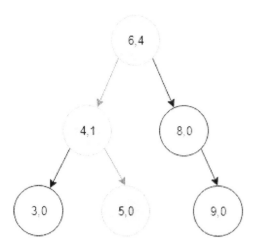

Now we can see that lcount of current node is equal to k therefore, return the value of that node which is our output.

Insight:

A BST is built to find the smallest or the largest element, but the structure is such that we can find the kth smallest element as well. This is not true in other data structures that we may develop.

Can you find the first k smallest elements? by extending our approach. We will answer in the next problem.

Sum of k smallest elements in Binary Search Tree

Given a binary search tree and an integer k, our task is to find that sum of all elements which is less or equal to the kth smallest element in binary search tree.

For example, for given below binary search tree and k=3.

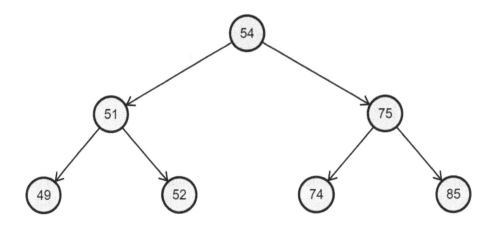

Explanation: In above example, k^{th} smallest element is 52 and sum of all the elements which is less or equal to 52 is 152.

We will explore two approaches:

- Naive approach O(N)
- Efficient approach O(log N)

Naive Approach

This is a simple approach this takes O(n) time and O(1) extra space.

Algorithm:

- Do inorder traversal of binary search tree and count the visited elements and add all the elements to a variable.

278

- When count is equal to k return the variable having sum of all the elements until that point and that is the output.

Implementation of above algorithm in C++ is given below:

```cpp
// function return sum of all element smaller than
// and equal to Kth smallest element
int ksmallestElementSumRec(Node *root, int k, int &count)
{
        // Base cases
        if (root == NULL)
                return 0;
        if (count > k)
                return 0;

        // Compute sum of elements in left subtree
        int res = ksmallestElementSumRec(root->left, k, count);
        if (count >= k)
                return res;

        // Add root's data
        res += root->data;

        // Add current Node
        count++;
        if (count == k)
        return res;

        // If count is less than k, return right subtree Nodes
        return res + ksmallestElementSumRec(root->right,
                k, count);
}

// Wrapper over ksmallestElementSumRec()
int ksmallestElementSum(struct Node *root, int k)
{
    int count = 0;
    ksmallestElementSumRec(root, k, count);
}
```

279

Explanation:

First of all, go to the left most element and add to the variable. In this case, it is res and increment the counter by 1. So, now res = 49 and count = 1. Now, check if count is equal to three. If no, then go another element.

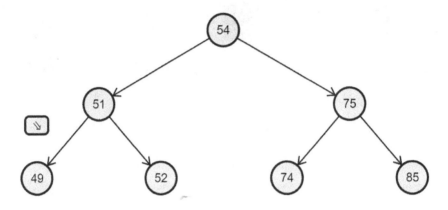

Now current node is 51 add it to the res and increase counter by 1 now res = 100 and count = 2, check if count is not equal to k, then go to the another element.

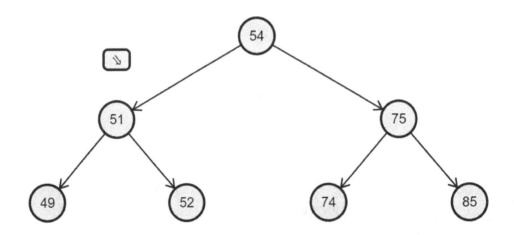

Now current node is 52 add it to the res and increase counter by 1 now res = 152 and count = 3 check if count if equal to k yes then return res and it is required output.

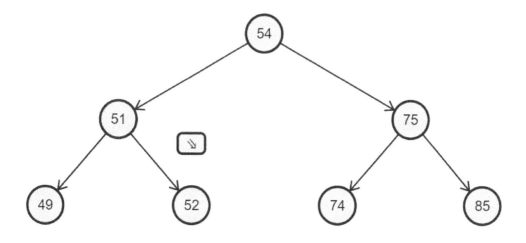

Efficient Approach

Here we use augmented tree data structure to solve this problem efficiently in O(h) time [h is height of Binary Search Tree] .

Structure of Augmented Tree

Binary Search Tree Node contain to extra fields : lCount , Sum

For each Node of Binary Search Tree

- lCount : store how many left child it has
- Sum : store sum of all left child it has

The node is as follows:

```
/* Binary tree node */
struct node
{
    int data;
```

```
    int lCount;

    node* left;
    node* right;
};
```

Insertion in Augmented Tree

When we insert a node in this tree if key value is less, then current node value then, add key value to the sum of the current node and increment lcount by 1 of that node. if key value is greater than current node then, go to the right similar to binary tree.

Do above process to all he nodes which come in the way till you do not reach the insertion point.

For example: binary search tree given below; we want insert 49 in it.

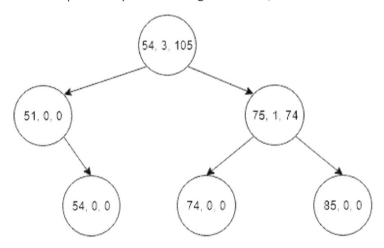

Now tree becomes as shown below.

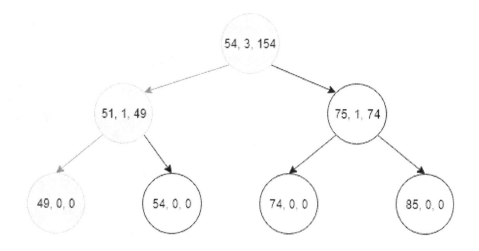

Following is the pseudocode to insert an element into our augmented BST:

```
/* Iterative insertion
   Recursion is least preferred unless we gain something
*/
node *insert(node *root, int data)
{
    node *node_t = newNode(data);
    /* A crawling pointer */
    node *pTraverse = root;
    node *currentParent = root;

    // Traverse till appropriate node
    while(pTraverse)
    {
        currentParent = pTraverse;

        if( node_t->data < pTraverse->data )
        {
            /* We are branching to left subtree
               increment node count */
            pTraverse->lCount++;
            /* left subtree */
            pTraverse = pTraverse->left;
        }
        else
        {
            /* right subtree */
```

```
            pTraverse = pTraverse->right;
        }
    }

    /* If the tree is empty, make it as root node */
    if( !root )
    {
        root = node_t;
    }
    else if( node_t->data < currentParent->data )
    {
        /* Insert on left side */
        currentParent->left = node_t;
    }
    else
    {
        /* Insert on right side */
        currentParent->right = node_t;
    }

    return root;
}
```

Algorithm for finding sum of k smallest elements in Binary Search Tree

```
Find Kth smallest element
[ temp_sum store sum of all element less than equal to K ]


ksmallestElementSumRec(root, K, temp_sum)


  IF root -> lCount == K + 1

      temp_sum += root->data + root->sum;

      break;

  ELSE

      IF k > root->lCount    // Goto right sub-tree

          temp_sum += root->data + root-> sum;
```

```
        ksmallestElementSumRec(root->right, K-root->lcount+1,
temp_sum)
    ELSE
        // Goto left sun-tree
        ksmallestElementSumRec( root->left, K, temp_sum)
```

Implementation of above algorithm is given below.

```
// function return sum of all element smaller than and equal
// to Kth smallest element
void ksmallestElementSumRec(Node *root, int k , int &temp_sum)
{
        if (root == NULL)
                return ;

        // if we fount k smallest element then break the
function
        if ((root->lCount + 1) == k)
        {
                temp_sum += root->data + root->Sum ;
                return ;
        }

        else if (k > root->lCount)
        {
                // store sum of all element smaller than current
root ;
                temp_sum += root->data + root->Sum;

                // decremented k and call right sub-tree
                k = k -( root->lCount + 1);
                ksmallestElementSumRec(root->right , k ,
temp_sum);
        }
        else // call left sub-tree
                ksmallestElementSumRec(root->left , k , temp_sum
);
}
```

285

```
// Wrapper over ksmallestElementSumRec()
int ksmallestElementSum(struct Node *root, int k)
{
        int sum = 0;
        ksmallestElementSumRec(root, k, sum);
        return sum;
}
```

Explanation:

First of all, go to the root and compare k with lcount + 1 if it is equal then temp_sum = 208 and return otherwise if k < lCount then go the left child of the root.

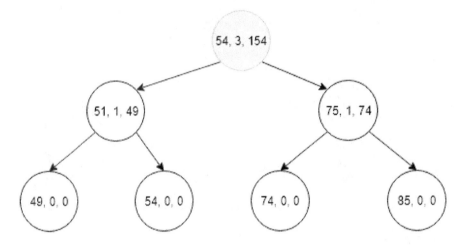

Now compare the lCount + 1 of current node with k if it is equal then temp_sum = 100 and return if k>lCount the go to right and temp_sum = 100 and k = 1.

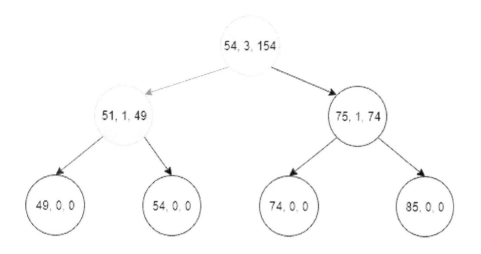

Now again compare lCount + 1 with k if it is equal then temp_sum = 152 and return.

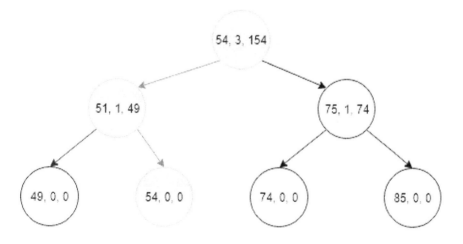

- Time Complexity: **O(log N)**

If we have our augmented Tree ready, we can find the sum of first K smallest elements in O(logN) time as in the worst case, we have to traverse to a leaf node.

- Space Complexity: **O(N)**

The space complexity is O(N) as we have augmented our Binary Search Tree and store extra attributes for each node.

Insight:

This problem shows that a Data Structure can go beyond its power if it stores extra information. You can imagine that if we store all information, a specific Data Structure can be taken to the edge. This brings in significant space overhead, so Data Structure are tuned according to the problem at hand.

You can imagine this as different species of the same Data Structure.

Different Self Balancing Binary Trees

A self-balancing binary tree is a Binary tree that automatically keeps its height small in the face of arbitrary insertions and deletions on the tree. The height is usually maintained in the order of **log n** (optimal) so that all operations performed on that tree take **O(log n)** time on an average. Let us look at the most widely used self-balancing binary trees, their complexities and their use cases. The various self-balancing binary search trees are:

- 2-3 tree
- Red-Black Tree
- AVL tree
- B tree
- AA tree
- Scapegoat Tree
- Splay tree
- Treap
- Weight Balanced trees

1. 2-3 Tree

A 2-3 tree is a self-balancing binary tree data structure where each node in the tree has either:

- 2 children and 1 data element.
- 3 children and 2 data elements.

Leaf nodes are at the same level and have no children but have either 1 or 2 data elements.

An example of a 2-3 tree is shown below.

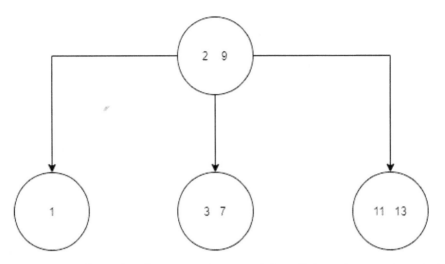

You can see from the above tree that it satisfies all the rules mentioned above.

Time Complexity in Big O notation:

The time complexity for average and worst case is the same for a 2-3 tree i.e.

- Space - O(n)
- Search - O(log n)
- Insert - O(log n)
- Delete - O(log n)

2. Red-Black Tree

A Red-Black tree is another self-balancing binary search tree. Each node stores an extra bit which represents the color which is used to ensure that the tree remains balanced during the insertion and deletion operations. Every node has the following rules in addition to that imposed by a binary search tree:

- Every node is either colored red or black.
- Root of the tree is always black.
- All leaves that is NIL are always black.
- There are no two adjacent red nodes that is a red node cannot have a red child or a red parent.
- Every path from a node to any of its descendant NIL node has the same number of black nodes.

290

Below is an example of a red-black tree.

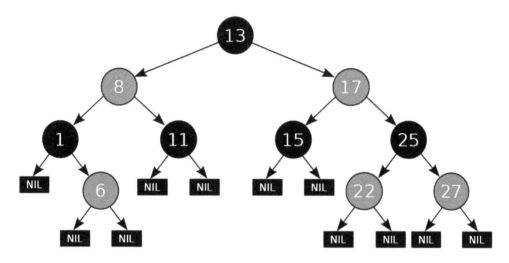

Time Complexity in Big O notation:

The time complexity for average and worst case is the same for a red-black tree i.e.

- Space - O(n)
- Search - O(log n)
- Insert - O(log n)
- Delete - O(log n)

3. AVL Tree

AVL tree is a type of self-balancing binary search tree where the difference between heights of the left and right subtrees cannot be more than one for all nodes in the tree. This is called the Balance Factor and is defined to be:

BalanceFactor(node) = Height(RightSubTree(node)) - Height(LeftSubTree(node))

which is an integer from the set {-1, 0, 1} if it is an AVL tree.

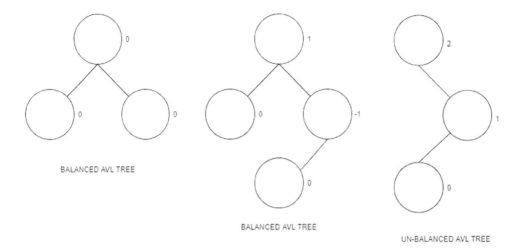

BALANCED AVL TREE   BALANCED AVL TREE   UN-BALANCED AVL TREE

Time Complexity in Big O notation:

The time complexity for an AVL tree is as shown below

- Space - O(n)
- Search - O(log n)
- Insert - O(log n)
- Delete - O(log n)

4. B-tree

A B-Tree is a type of self-balancing binary search tree which generalizes the binary search tree, allowing for nodes with more than 2 children.

A B-tree of order m is a tree which satisfies the following properties:

- Every node has at most m children.
- Every non-leaf node (except root) has at least ⌈m/2⌉ child nodes.
- The root has at least two children if it is not a leaf node.
- A non-leaf node with k children contains k − 1 keys.
- All leaves appear in the same level and carry no information.

Below is an example of a B-Tree:

292

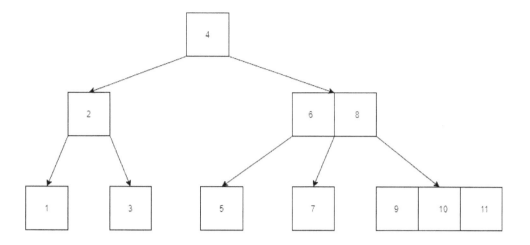

A B-Tree of order 3 is a 2-3 Tree. Can you imagine this?

Time Complexity in Big O notation:

The time complexity for a B-Tree (Average and Worst Case) shown below

- Space - O(n)
- Search - O(log n)
- Insert - O(log n)
- Delete - O(log n)

Applications of B-Trees:

- Well suited for storage systems that read and write relatively large block of data.
- Used in databases and file systems.

5. AA Tree

Unlike in red-black trees, red nodes on an AA tree can only be added as a right sub-child that is no red node can be a left sub-child. The following five invariants hold for AA trees:

- The level of every leaf node is one.

- The level of every left child is exactly one less than that of its parent.
- The level of every right child is equal to or one less than that of its parent.
- The level of every right grandchild is strictly less than that of its grandparent.
- Every node of level greater than one, has two children.

Below is an example of an AA tree.

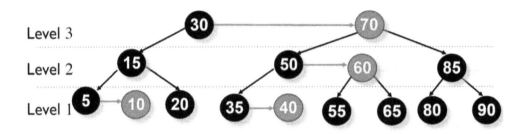

It guarantees fast operations in **O(log n)** time, and the implementation code is perhaps the shortest among all the balanced trees.

6. Scapegoat Tree

A scapegoat tree is a self-balancing variant of the binary search tree. Unlike other self-balancing trees, scapegoat tree does not require any extra storage per node of the tree. The low overhead and easy implementation make the scapegoat tree a very attractive option as a self-balancing binary search tree.

The balancing idea is to make sure that nodes are α (alpha) size balanced. What this means is that the sizes of left and right subtrees are at most α times (size of node) that is **α * (size of node)**. This concept is based on the fact that if a node is α weight balanced, it is also height balanced with height less than $\log\_(1/\alpha)(size + 1)$.

Time Complexity in Big O notation (Average Case) :

The time complexity for a Scapegoat tree for average case is as shown below

- Space - O(n)
- Search - O(log n)
- Insert - O(log n)

294

- Delete - O(log n)

Time Complexity in Big O notation (Worst Case) : The time complexity for a Scapegoat tree for worst case is as shown below

- Space - O(n)
- Search - O(log n)
- Insert - amortized O(log n)
- Delete - amortized O(log n)

7. Splay tree

A splay tree is a self-balancing binary search tree with the additional property that recently accessed elements are quick to access again. All normal operations on a binary tree are combined with one basic operation called splaying. Splaying of the tree for a certain element rearranges the tree so that the element is placed at the root of the tree.

For example, when you perform a standard binary search for an element in question, and then use the tree rotations in a specific order such that this element is now placed as the root. We could also make use of a top-down algorithm to combine the search and the reorganization into a single phase.

Splaying depends on three different factors when we try to access an element called x:

- whether x is the left or right child of its parent node p
- whether p is the root or not, and if not
- whether p is the left or right child of its parent g (the grandparent of x)

Based on this, we have three different types of operations:

Zig: This step is done when p is the root.

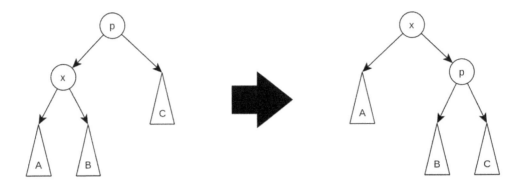

Zig-Zig: This step is done when p is not the root and x and p are either both right children or are both left children.

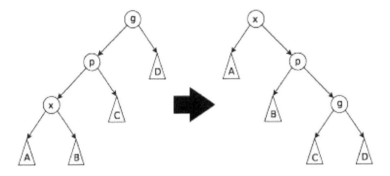

Zag-Zig: This is done when p is not the root and x is a right child and p is a left child or vice versa.

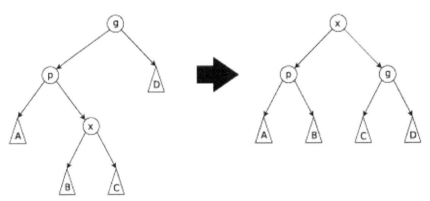

Time Complexity in Big O notation (Average Case) : The time complexity for the search, insert and delete operations in average case is **O(log n)**.

Time Complexity in Big O notation (Worst Case) : The time complexity for a Splay tree for worst case is as follows:

- Space - O(n)
- Search - amortized O(log n)
- Insert - amortized O(log n)
- Delete - amortized O(log n)

8. Treap

Treap is a data structure that combines both a binary tree and a binary heap, but it does not guarantee to have a height of **O(log n)**. The concept is to use randomization and binary heap property to maintain balance with high probability.

Every node of a treap contains 2 values:

- **KEY** which follows standard binary search tree ordering.
- **PRIORITY** which is a randomly assigned value that follows max-heap property.

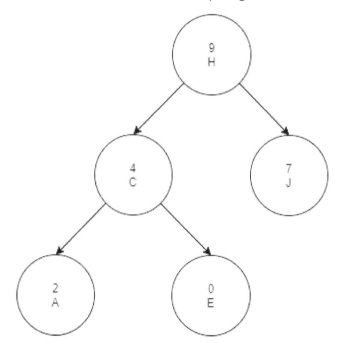

The above example is a treap with alphabetic key and numeric max heap order.

Treap support the following basic operations:

- To search for a given key value, apply a standard binary search algorithm in a binary search tree, ignoring the priorities.
- To insert a new key x into the treap, generate a random priority y for x. Binary search for x in the tree, and create a new node at the leaf position where the binary search determines a node for x should exist. Then, as long as x is not the root of the tree and has a larger priority number than its parent z, perform a tree rotation that reverses the parent-child relation between x and z.
- To delete a node x from the treap, if x is a leaf of the tree, simply remove it. If x has a single child z, remove x from the tree and make z be the child of the parent of x (or make z the root of the tree if x had no parent). Finally, if x has two children, swap its position in the tree with the position of its immediate successor z in the sorted order, resulting in one of the previous cases. In this final case, the swap may violate the heap-ordering property for z, so additional rotations may be needed to be performed to restore this property.

Time Complexity in Big O notation (Average Case) :

The time complexity for a Treap for average case is as shown below

- Space - O(n)
- Search - O(log n)
- Insert - O(log n)
- Delete - O(log n)

Time Complexity in Big O notation (Worst Case) :

The time complexity for a Treap for worst case is as shown below

- Space - O(n)
- Search - O(n)
- Insert - O(n)
- Delete - O(n)

298

9. Weight Balanced trees

Weight-balanced trees are binary search trees, which can be used to implement finite sets and finite maps. Although other balanced binary search trees such as AVL trees and red-black trees use height of subtrees for balancing, the balance of WBTs is **based on the sizes of the subtrees** below each node.

The **size of a tree is the number of associations** that it contains. Weight-balanced binary trees are balanced to keep the sizes of the subtrees of each node within a constant factor of each other.

This ensures logarithmic times for single-path operations (like lookup and insertion). A weight-balanced tree takes space that is proportional to the number of associations in the tree.

A node of a WBT has the fields

- key of any ordered type
- value (optional) for mappings
- left and right pointer to nodes
- size of integer type

At this point, you must have the idea that there are several types of Self-balancing Binary Search Trees and each has an unique approach to keep the tree balanced.

Insight

Self-balancing BSTs are flexible data structures, in that it is easy to extend them to efficiently record additional information or perform new operations. For example, one can record the number of nodes in each subtree having a certain property, allowing one to count the number of nodes in a certain key range with that property in O(log n) time. These extensions can be used, for example, to optimize database queries or other list-processing algorithms.

299

We will cover AVL Tree and Splay Tree in depth so that you have a clear idea of a couple of ways we can make sure that our Binary Tree is balanced. These two tree data structures give you a strong foundation and are similar to other common data structures we listed in terms of usage.

AVL Tree

An **AVL Tree (Adelson-Velsky and Landis tree)** is a self-balancing binary search tree such that for every internal node of the tree, the heights of the children of node can differ by at most 1. If the difference **in** the height of left and right sub-trees is more than 1, the tree is **balanced using rotation techniques**.

The credit of AVL Tree goes to **Georgy Adelson-Velsky** and **Evgenii Landis**.

Every node in an AVL tree has a number known as balance factor associated with it.

BalanceFactor = height of right-subtree – height of left-subtree

In an AVL Tree, **balance_factor** is an integer from the set **{-1, 0, 1}**.

If it is different from the three integers, the tree needs to be balanced using techniques we will discuss further.

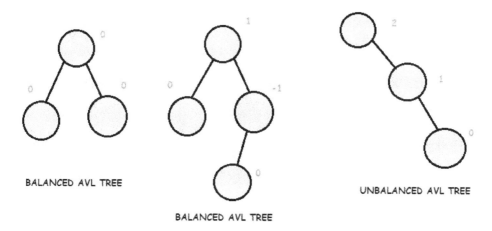

BALANCED AVL TREE

BALANCED AVL TREE

UNBALANCED AVL TREE

The node definition in an AVL Tree is as follows:

```
struct Node
{
    int _data;
    Node *left;
    Node *right;
```

```
        int _height;
};
```

To make itself balanced, an AVL tree may perform four kinds of rotations:

- Left rotation (LL Rotation)
- Right rotation (RR Rotation)
- Left-Right rotation (LR Rotation)
- Right-Left rotation (RL Rotation)

Left rotation (LL Rotation) and Right rotation (RR Rotation) are single rotations while Left-Right rotation (LR Rotation) and Right-Left rotation (RL Rotation) are double rotations.

We can find the height of each node using the following function implementation:

```
int Height (Node*node)
{
    if (node==nullptr)
        return 0;
    int lh=Height(node->left);
    int rh=Height(node->right);
    if (lh > rh)
        return lh+1;
    else
        return rh+1;
}
```

Following function implementation will check if a node is correctly balanced:

```
int getBalance (Node *node)
{
    if (node==nullptr)
        return 0;
    return Height(node->left) - Height(node->right);
}
```

302

Following are the details regarding the various rotation techniques employed by AVL tree:

1. Left Rotation

A left rotation is a balancing technique that is applied on an unbalanced AVL Tree on a node having the balance_factor > 1. The unbalance property can be triggered by an insertion or deletion in a balanced AVL Tree.

In Left Rotation, every node moves one position to left from the current position.

Consider the following example:

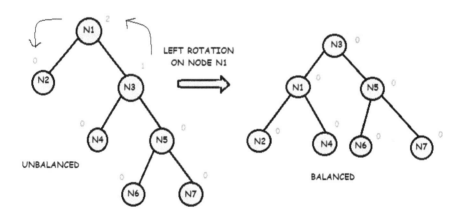

Notice that node N3 takes the place of node N1. N1 takes the place of node N2 and becomes the left child of node N3. Node N2 becomes the left child of node N1. Node N4, which was the left child of node N3, becomes the right child of node N1.

Note that nodes N2 and N4 can be replaced by subtrees.

This operation takes O(log N) time complexity in the worst-case scenario.

303

The left rotation operation can be implemented as follows:

```
Node *getLeftRotate (Node *x)
{
    Node *y=x->right;
    Node *T2=y->left;
    y->left=x;
    x->right=T2;
    x->_height=std::max(Height(x->left),Height(x->right))+1;
    y->_height=std::max(Height(y->left),Height(y->right))+1;
    return y;
}
```

2.Right Rotation

A right rotation is a balancing technique that is applied on an unbalanced AVL Tree on a node having the balance_factor < -1. The unbalance property can be triggered by an insertion or deletion in a balanced AVL Tree.

In Right Rotation, every node moves one position to right from the current position.

Consider the following example:

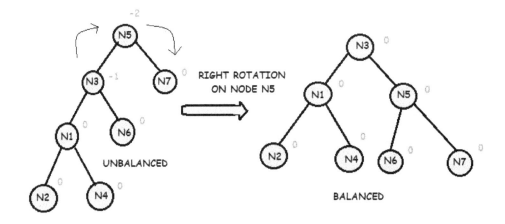

304

Notice that node N3 takes the place of node N5. N1 takes the original place of node N3 and becomes the left child of node N3. Node N6, which was the right child of node N3, becomes the left child of node N5.

Note that nodes N1 and N6 can be replaced by subtrees.

This operation takes O(log N) time complexity in the worst-case scenario.

The right rotation operation can be implemented as follows:

```
Node *getRightRotate (Node *y)
{
    Node *x=y->left;
    Node *T2=x->right;
    x->right=y;
    y->left=T2;
    y->_height=std::max(Height(y->left) , Height(y->right))+1;
    x->_height=std::max(Height(x->left) , Height(x->right))+1;
    return x;
}
```

3. Left Right Rotation

The Left Right Rotation is combination of single left rotation followed by single right rotation. In LR Rotation, first every node moves one position to left then one position to right from the current position.

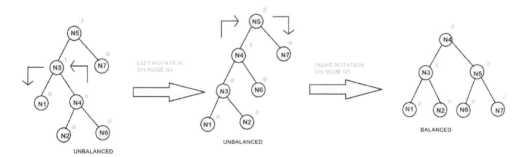

4. Right Left Rotation

The Right Left Rotation is combination of single right rotation followed by single left rotation. In RL Rotation, first every node moves one position to right then one position to left from the current position.

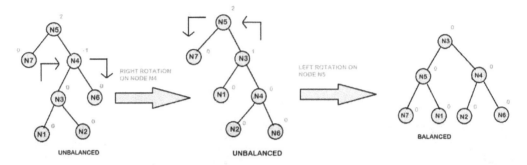

How to choose a particular rotation?

A tree rotation is necessary when you have inserted or deleted a node which leaves the tree in an unbalanced state. An unbalanced state is defined as a state in which any subtree has a balance factor of greater than 1, or less than -1. That is, any tree with a difference between the heights of its two subtrees greater than 1, is considered unbalanced.

- Get the balance factor (left subtree height – right subtree height) of the current node.
- If balance factor is greater than 1, then the current node is unbalanced and we are either in Left case or left Right case. To check whether it is left case or not, compare the newly inserted key with the key in left subtree root.
- If balance factor is less than -1, then the current node is unbalanced and we are either in Right case or Right Left case. To check whether it is Right case or not, compare the newly inserted key with the key in right subtree root.

Pseudocode for Insert

Pseudocode of AVL Tree insert operation is as follows:

- Insert as in a Binary Search Tree.
- Check back up path for imbalance, which will be 1 of 4 cases:

306

1. node's left-left grandchild is too tall

2. node's left-right grandchild is too tall

3. node's right-left grandchild is too tall

4. node's right-right grandchild is too tall

- Only one case occurs because tree was balanced before insert
- After the appropriate single or double rotation: the smallest unbalanced subtree has the same height as before the insertion
- So, all ancestors are now balanced

Example:

This is an example of building an AVL Tree by inserting 4,5,6,7,16 and 15 sequentially to an, initially, balanced binary search tree with 3 nodes (1,2,3)):

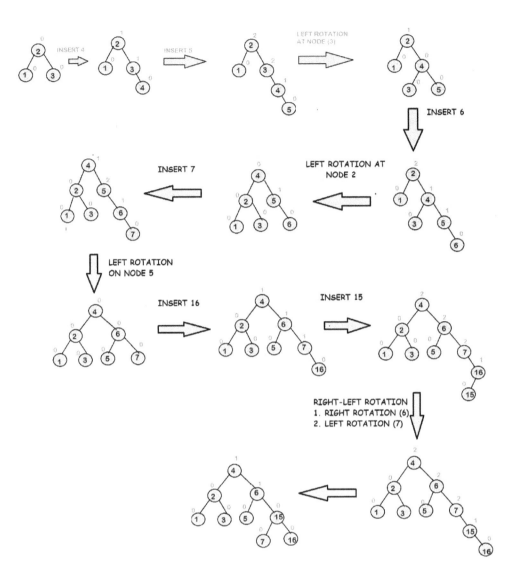

The insert function implementation will be as follows:

```
Node* insertToAVL (Node*node, int _data)
{
    if(node==NULL)
        return NewNode(_data);
    if(_data < node->_data)
    {
```

```
          node->left=insertToAVL(node->left,_data);
     }
     else if(_data > node->_data)
     {
          node->right=insertToAVL(node->right,_data);
     }
     else
     {
          return node;
     }
     node->_height=1+std::max(Height(node->left),Height(node-
>right));
     int balance = getBalance(node);
     //left left rotation
     if(balance > 1 && _data < node->left->_data)
     {
          return getRightRotate(node);
     }
     // right right rotation
     if(balance < -1 && _data > node->right->_data)
     {
          return getLeftRotate(node);
     }
     //left Right Rotation
     if(balance > 1 && _data > node->left->_data)
     {
          node->left=getLeftRotate(node->left);
          return getRightRotate(node);
     }
     //Right Left Rotation
     if(balance < -1 && _data < node->right->_data)
     {
          node->right=getRightRotate(node->right);
          return getLeftRotate(node);
     }
     return node;
}
```

Complexity

- Worst case time complexity for search operation: O(log N)
- Worst case time complexity for insert operation: O(log N)

- Worst case time complexity to build tree : O(N log N)

Insight:

With AVL Tree, you got an idea how the structure of nodes are modified if we want to keep our Binary Tree balanced. Notice that we added the restriction of keeping our Binary Tree balanced but it did not impact the complexity performance.

Can you imagine (based on the problems we solved) for which restrictions, fundamental operations face a setback or overload?

Splay Tree

Splay tree is a Self-adjusting Binary Tree with additional property that recently accessed elements as kept near the top and hence, are quick to access next time. After performing operations, the tree gets adjusted/ modified and this modification of tree is called *Splaying*.

Why Splaying?

The frequently accessed elements move closer to root so that they can be accessed quickly. Having frequently used nodes near the root is useful for implementing cache and garbage collection as the access time is reduced significantly for real-time performance.

Splaying

Whenever a node is accessed, a splaying operation is performed on that node. This is a sequence of operations done on the node which sequentially brings up that node closer to root and eventually makes it as root of that tree. Now, if we want to access that same node from the tree, then the time complexity will be **O(1)**. This is what we mean by frequently accessed elements are easily accessible in less time.

We will explain the exact steps further into this chapter.

Insertion in Splay Tree

Pseudocode

- If root is NULL, we allocate a new node and return it as root of the tree.
- Check for insertion location by searching the tree for the parent.
- After finding parent node link the new node with that node and perform Splaying operation which makes new node as root of the tree.

```
12 -> 6 -> 2 -> 5 -> 13 -> 4
```

The Image does not include rotation step. This is just simple insertion operation for a BST.

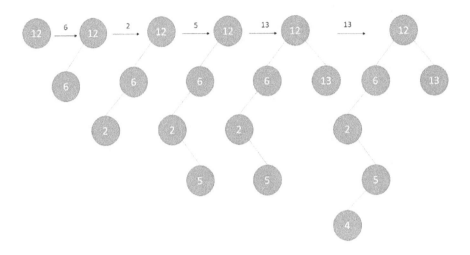

Following is the pseudocode for insert operation:

```
Insert(T,n)
    temp = T.root
    y = NULL
    while temp is not equal to NULL{
        y = temp
        if n.data < temp.data
                    temp = temp.left
        else temp = temp.right
    }
    n.parent = y
    # Check if Tree is empty. If empty, then make n as root of tree
    if y == NULL
        T.root = n
    else if n.data < y.data
        y.left = n
    else y.right = n
        Splay(T,n)
```

When we call Insert on an empty tree, the data is made to be root node of the tree.

312

Then we call another Insert function, now it will assign temp variable as T.root. and y as NULL.

Checks while loop condition. As new temp variable is not empty, it enters loop.

Assigns y = temp (temp is root now)

Checks if n.data is less than temp.data that is compares the new data with the node in tree. If new data to be inserted is less than the tree node then temp = temp.left (updates temp as its pointer to left child).

If n.data is greater than temp.data update temp as temp.right

Now it will come out of loop because the left or right child pointers to the root node is empty that is it falsifies the condition temp != NULL.

Assigns n.parent = y. (y is the updated pointer to the child of temp)

Checking if n.data < y.data. If n is less than y value then assign y.left = n

else y.right = n

Call Splay operation.

We will first define class Node.

```python
class Node:
    def __init__(self, data):
        self.data = data
        self.parent = None
        self.left = None
        self.right = None
```

Following is the implementation of Insert operation in Python:

```python
def insert(self, key):
    # This is a class Node used to create new node.
    node =   Node(key)
    y = None
    x = self.root
```

313

```
while x != None:
    y = x
    if node.data < x.data:
        x = x.left
    else:
        x = x.right

# y is parent of x
node.parent = y
if y == None:
    self.root = node
elif node.data < y.data:
    y.left = node
else:
    y.right = node
# splay the node
self.__splay(node)
```

Splaying Operation

Let the node to be accessed be x and parent of that node be p. Let grandparent of x be g. (parent of node p)

Depends upon 3 factors:

- If the node x is left child or right child of its parent node p.
- If the parent node p is root node or not.
- If the parent node is left child or right child of its parent node that is grandparent of node x.

Zig step (right rotation)

This step is done when parent node of inserted node is root node of the tree.

Zig-Zig step (double right rotation)

314

When parent node of inserted node is not the root node. And if the inserted node is left child of its parent node and that parent node is left child of its parent node then perform zig zig operation.

Similarly Zag Zag operation is performed if the inserted node is the right child of its parent node and that parent node is the right child of its parent node.

```
ZigZig rotation(right-right)
      G                              P                                    X
     / \                           / \                                   / \
    P   T4   rightRotate(G)    X       G      rightRotate(P)   T1    P
   / \       ============>    / \     / \     ============>          / \
  X   T3                     T1 T2   T3 T4                          T2   G
 / \                                                                    / \
T1 T2                                                                  T3   T4


ZagZag rotation(left-left rotation)

  G                              P                              X
 / \                            / \                            / \
T1  P      leftRotate(G)    G       X      leftRotate(P)    P    T4
   / \     ============>   / \     / \     ============>   / \
  T2  X                  T1 T2   T3 T4                    G    T3
     / \                                                 / \
    T3 T4                                               T1   T2
```

Zig-Zag step (right and left rotation)

Performed if parent node is not the root node and x is right child of its parent and that parent node is left child of its parent node.

If x is root node, then there is no need to perform Splay operation.

315

```
Zag-Zig (Left Right Case):
      G                           G                               X
     / \                         / \                             / \
    P   T4   leftRotate(P)      X   T4   rightRotate(G)          P   G
   / \       ============>     / \       ============>          / \ / \
  T1  X                       P  T3                            T1 T2 T3 T4
     / \                     / \
    T2 T3                   T1  T2

Zig-Zag (Right Left Case):
    G                           G                               X
   / \                         / \                             / \
  T1  P    rightRotate(P)     T1  X    leftRotate(P)          G   P
     / \   ============>         / \   ============>         / \ / \
    X   T4                      T2  P                        T1 T2 T3 T4
   / \                             / \
  T2 T3                           T3  T4
```

Example:

```
      100                       100                    [20]
     /  \                      /  \                        \
    50  200                   50  200                      50
   /         search(20)      /        search(20)          /  \
  40         ======>        [20]      ========>          30  100
  /          1. Zig-Zig        \      2. Zig-Zig           \    \
 30          at 40             30     at 100               40  200
 /                              \
[20]                           40
```

Pseudocode

Enter in while loop if parent of node x is not None.

Check if grandparent of node is None. This means our node is at 2nd level. If it is at 2nd level, then again check if its right child or left child. If its left child performs right rotation or if its right child, then perform left rotation.

Condition to check if both the parent and grandparent of node x exists and are left children of their parent nodes.

(x == x.parent.left and x.parent == x.parent.parent.left)

If true, then perform right rotation on grandparent first then parent. This is Zig Zig condition.

Condition to check if both the parent and grandparent of node x exists and are right children of their parent nodes.

(x == x.parent.right and x.parent == x.parent.parent.right)

ZagZag condition.

Check x == x.parent.right and x.parent == x.parent.parent.left this conditions checks if the parent node is right child and this parent node is left child of "its" parent node. First perform left rotation on parent then right rotation on grandparent. (Zig Zag condition)

Opposite case will be for Zag Zig condition. Perform right rotation on parent node. then left rotation on grandparent.

```python
def __splay(self, x):
    #performed when node is not root node
    while x.parent != None:
        #Zig or Zag condition
        if x.parent.parent == None:
            #Zig condition # zig rotation
            if x == x.parent.left:
                self.__right_rotate(x.parent)
            else:
                # zag rotation
                self.__left_rotate(x.parent)
        #ZigZig
        elif x == x.parent.left and \
                x.parent == x.parent.parent.left:
            # zig-zig rotation
```

317

```
            #rotate grandparent of x to right
            self.__right_rotate(x.parent.parent)
            #then rotate parent node to right
            self.__right_rotate(x.parent)
        elif x == x.parent.right and
              x.parent == x.parent.parent.right:
    #ZagZag zag-zag rotation
            self.__left_rotate(x.parent.parent)
            self.__left_rotate(x.parent)
        elif x == x.parent.right and
              x.parent == x.parent.parent.left:
            #ZigZag zig-zag rotation
            #rotate parent to left
            self.__left_rotate(x.parent)
            #rotate updated x to right
            self.__right_rotate(x.parent)
        else:
            # zag-zig rotation
            self.__right_rotate(x.parent)
            self.__left_rotate(x.parent)
```

Above code performs multiple Zig-Zag or ZigZig operations until the target node does not become a root node.

Right rotation

```
    x                                         y
   / \      Zig (Right Rotation)            / \
  y   T3   - - - - - - - - - ->           T1   x
 / \        < - - - - - - - -                 / \
T1  T2      Zag (Left Rotation)             T2   T3
```

Observing the rotation, we can see that right child of x is now left child of x and y becomes root node.

In right rotation, reverse of the left rotation happens.

318

Pseudocode:

- Assign left child of x to y.
- Make right child of y as left child of x.
- Check if right child of y is not None. Make T2 as right child of x.
- Check if parent of x is None. Make y as root node.
- Else if x is a right child, then make y as right child of x.
- Else make y as left child of x.
- Make x as y's right child.
- Make y as x's parent node.

```python
def __right_rotate(self, x):
    y = x.left
    x.left = y.right
    if y.right != None:
        y.right.parent = x

    y.parent = x.parent;
    if x.parent == None:
        self.root = y
    elif x == x.parent.right:
        x.parent.right = y
    else:
        x.parent.left = y

    y.right = x
    x.parent = y
```

Left rotation (Zag)

Pseudocode:

- Assign right child of x to y.
- Make left child of y as right child of x.
- Check if left child of y is not None. Make T2 as left child of x.
- Check if parent of x is None. Make y as root node.
- Else if x is a left child then make y as left child of x.
- Else make y as right child of x.

319

- Make x as y's left child.
- Make y as x's parent node.

```python
def __left_rotate(self, x):
        y = x.right
        x.right = y.left
        if y.left != None:
                y.left.parent = x
        y.parent = x.parent
        if x.parent == None:
                self.root = y
        elif x == x.parent.left:
                x.parent.left = y
        else:
                x.parent.right = y
        y.left = x
        x.parent = y
```

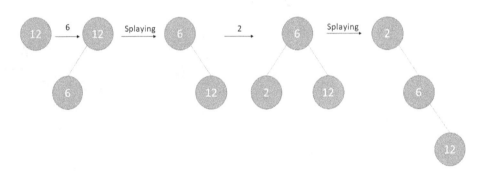

Deletion in Splay Tree

Deletion can be done using Top-Down approach.

Let the node to be deleted be x.

First step in deletion is to find the element that has to be deleted in our tree.

Now there could be 2 conditions possible, which are if the key is found and if it is not found.

We will traverse the tree till the key is found, and when it is not found, we will eventually reach to the end that is leaf node. So, now perform Splay operation and return that key is not found.

Pseudocode

1. Search node to be deleted.

2. Return something if key is not found.

3. Perform splay operation on that key.

4. Unlink that key node from its parent and its children, causing the tree to split into 2 subtrees.

5. Call Join function.

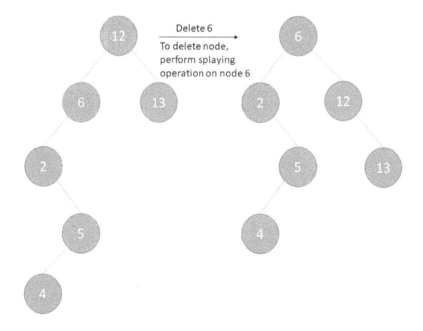

While traversing, if the key is found in the tree, then perform Splaying which makes the node as the root of tree as shown in the figure. Now, the node to be deleted is root of the tree, so split the tree by unlinking the right and left child of x. Now, we will have 2 sub trees.

321

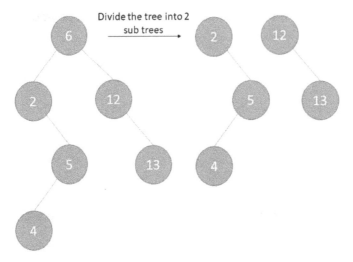

Divide the tree into 2 sub trees

Delete 6

Join the 2 trees using join operation, we will define join operation after deletion operation just to continue with the flow.

Following is the implementation in Python to perform deletion:

```python
def __delete_node_helper(self, node, key):
        x = None
        t = None
        s = None
        while node != None:    #searching node x to be deleted
                if node.data == key:
                        x = node
                if node.data <= key:
                        node = node.right
                else:
                        node = node.left

        if x == None: #If the node is not found then perform
splaying on the recently accessed node
                print "Couldn't find key in the tree"
                self.__splay(x)
                return
```

```
        # split operation
        self.__splay(x)    #if the key is found again perform
splaying on x
        #After splaying x is root node, check if the right child
of x is NULL
        if x.right != None:
            #if root.right is not NULL
            #t is temporary variable, assign t as right child of
x
                t = x.right
                t.parent = None  #unlinking x from its right
child
        else:        #If right child is empty then t = none
                t = None
        #3 steps to unlink x from its right child
        s = x
        s.right = None
        x = None
        #Now we have 2 trees, so join them
        if s.left != None:   #Check if left subtree is empty or
not
                s.left.parent = None    #Unlinking parent node
'x' from its left child
        self.root = self.__join(s.left, t)     #Perform join
operation on both trees
        s = None
```

Now let us define join operation

Note that even though the right subtree is empty we have to perform splay operation on the maximum element in left subtree

Join operation is done by finding the maximum value in left subtree, then splaying it.

323

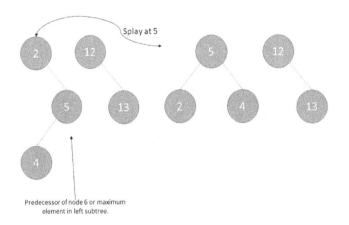

Delete 6

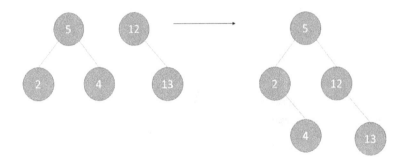

Pseudocode

1. If left subtree is empty then return right subtree as final tree. else perform 3rd step.

2. If right subtree is empty then still perform 3rd step.

3. Find maximum value node from the left subtree and perform splaying on that maximum node to bring it at the top.

4. Make the root of right subtree as the right child of root of the left subtree.

```
def __join(self, s, t):
#s is left subtree's root, t is right subtree's root
        if s == None:       #if left subtree is empty
                return t        #return right subtree as it is.
        if t == None:       #if right subtree is empty
            x = self.maximum(s)
            self.__splay(x)
            return x

        x = self.maximum(s)
        self.__splay(x)
        #pointing right child of x to t
        x.right = t
        #making parent of right child as x
        t.parent = x
        return x
```

If left subtree is empty, then we will simply return right subtree as it is.

Else if right subtree is empty then we will find the latest predecessor of our deleting node key by calling maximum function on left subtree which returns the greatest element from the left subtree. Then perform splaying operation on that element.

Else if both sub-trees are not empty, then find last predecessor of the node to be deleted or find the maximum value node in the left subtree, then splay it to bring that largest node to the top. Then link the root of right subtree as the right child of left subtree's root.

We have called maximum function in our code above. Because of the properties of BST, the implementation of maximum function is very easy, we just have to traverse to the right most child in our left subtree.

Pseudocode:

1. If right child of node is empty, return that node.

2. Else if right child is present then call the right child of that node again and again till node.right == None.

```
def maximum(self, node):
        while node.right != None:
                node = node.right
        return node
```

To find the **greatest element in a Binary search tree,** we will use its fundamental property that the right subtree of a node contains only nodes with keys greater than the node's key.

Using recursion, we will traverse towards the most rightward key of that tree. We first check if right child of a node is empty or not. If it is not empty, then traverse its right child again and again till our condition of node.right != None returns False.

Similarly for minimum function visit the most left node of the tree as the left subtree of a node contains only nodes with keys lesser than the node's key.

Pseudocode:

1. If left child of node is empty, return that node.

2. Else if left child exists then call the left child of that node till we reach leaf node that is node.left == None.

```
def minimum(self, node):
        while node.left != None:
                node = node.left
        return node
```

Traverse the left subtree till node.left returns None.

Search Operation

Pseudocode

1. Check if node to be find is none or key is equal to root node, then return that node as found.

2. If key to be found is less than node traverse left child recursively till we find the target key and reach leaf node.

3. If key is greater than node then traverse its right child till it is found and up to the leaf node.

Calling search function recursively

```python
def __search_tree_helper(self, node, key):
        if node == None or key == node.data:
                return node

        if key < node.data:
                return self.__search_tree_helper(node.left, key)
        return self.__search_tree_helper(node.right, key)
```

We will search an element according to the rules of BST. If the key is greater than node traverse its right child recursively, and if key is less than the node then traverses its left child recursively.

Inorder Traversal

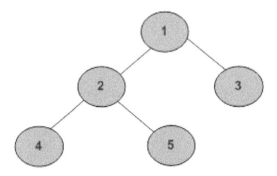

Inorder (Left, Root, Right) : 4 2 5 1 3

Pseudocode:

- Check if root node is None or not.
- If node is not empty then call inorder function again with its left child as argument. It checks again if node exist or not.
- Reach to the lowest level and print that node value if node has no children.
- Move back up (parent), print its value and explore its right subtree.
- Repeat step 4 till we reach root node.
- Start exploring right subtree and repeat from step 2 to 5.

Code:

```
def _in_order_helper(self, node):
        if node != None:
                self.__in_order_helper(node.left)
                #print its data and a blankspace
                sys.stdout.write(node.data + " ")
                self.__in_order_helper(node.right)
```

We are recursively traversing the left children of tree until we reach the leaf node then explore its right sibling then its parent node and its right sibling. Again, the parent node of current node is processed recursively. Then, we reach at the root node. We will now explore to the deepest of right subtree and print the leaf nodes values first then their parent repeatedly.

Successor and predecessor of a given node:

Successor

Pseudocode:

- Check if right child of root exists or not.
- If it exists, then call minimum function to find minimum value (We have already explained the maximum function).
- Successor is the left node of the right subtree of x.

```
def successor(self, x):
        # if the right subtree is not null,
        # the successor is the leftmost node in the
        # right subtree
        if x.right != None:
                return self.minimum(x.right)

        # else it is the lowest ancestor of x whose
        # left child is also an ancestor of x.
        y = x.parent
        while y != None and x == y.right:
                x = y
                y = y.parent
        return y
```

To find successor we will traverse its right subtree.

First check if right child exists or not, if it exists then we would want to find a minimum value node. For that we will call its left child in recursion until we reach the leaf node.

Predecessor

Pseudocode

- Check if left child exists or not.
- If it does then call minimum function on left subtree.
- (minimum function is already being covered)
- Predecessor is the rightmost node in left subtree.

```python
def predecessor(self, x):
        # if the left subtree is not null,
        # the predecessor is the rightmost node in the
        # left subtree
        if x.left != None:
                return self.maximum(x.left)

        y = x.parent
        while y != None and x == y.left:
                x = y
                y = y.parent
        return y
```

Predecessor is the maximum value node in the left subtree.

First check if left child exists or not, if it does then for finding the maximum value in left tree, we will explore the right children of root until we reach the right most node This is a leaf node.

With this, you have the complete knowledge of Splay Tree, a self-balancing Binary Tree (just like AVL Tree, Red Black Tree and others) but with an additional property.

Insight:

Splay Tree is important as it shows that we can impose multiple restrictions like self-balancing and recently accessed near the top and maintain the performance of simpler Binary Tree.

Think of what other features you want in your Self-balancing Binary Tree.

330

Binary Space Partitioning Trees

See this image:

On the left is Doom, a first-person shooter game that was released in 1993 which then, became a phenomenon. It is one of the most influential games of all time.

On the right is John Carmack, a genius video programmer, who ensured that the game is action-packed and frenetic!

Well, rendering a 3-D figure, is not something particularly challenging if you have all the time in the world, but a respectable time game, needs to be swift!

He made use of **Binary Space Partitioning** for its agility !

Introduced in the 1980s, this is a data structure of enormous potential.

As the name suggests, it refers to partitioning the space in a binary fashion, wherein it is key to be clear with what we mean by space

Space

N-dimensional space is a geometric setting in which N values (called parameters) are required to determine the position of an element (i.e., point).

Example

Two-dimensional space can be seen as a projection of the physical universe onto a plane.

331

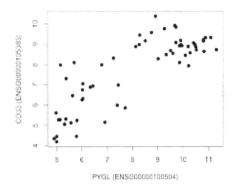

What is Binary Space partitioning?

It is a method of recursively subdividing a space into two convex sets by using hyperplanes as partitions. The resulting data structure is a binary tree, and the two sub-planes are referred to as front and back.

Example 1

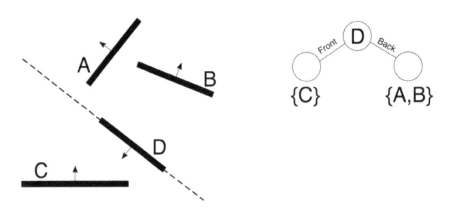

The root partitioning line is drawn along D, this splits the geometry in two sets as described in the tree.

332

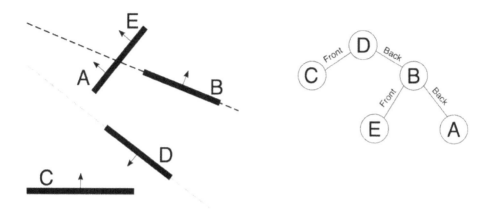

Further spaces have been split until no more splitting is required.

Example 2

The entire space is referred by the root node.

This is split by selecting a partition hyperplane.

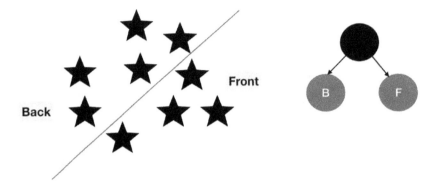

These two sub-planes, referred to as front and back contain more nodes, and hence shall be subdivided to get more sub-planes.

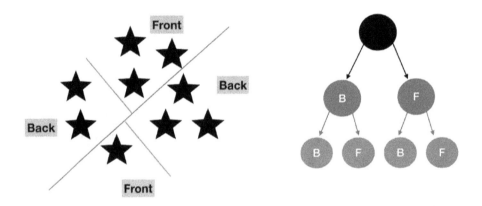

This process needs to be recursively repeated in every subspace created to finally render the complete binary tree where each leaf node contain distinct circles.

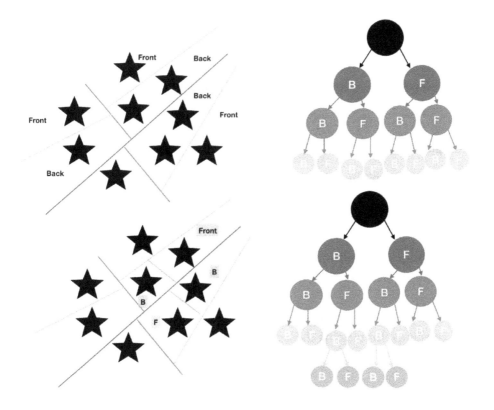

There we reach our Binary Space Partitioned Tree.

Algorithm for Common Operations

Generation

- Choose a polygon P from the list.
- Make a node N in the BSP tree and add P to the list of polygons at that node.
- For each other polygon in the list:
- If that polygon is wholly in front of the plane containing P then: move that polygon to the list of nodes in front of P.
- If that polygon is wholly behind the plane containing P then: move that polygon to the list of nodes behind P.
- If that polygon is intersected by the plane containing P then: split it into two polygons and move them to the respective lists of polygons behind and in front of P.

335

- If that polygon lies in the plane containing P then: add it to the list of polygons at node N.
- Apply this algorithm to the list of polygons in front of P.
- Apply this algorithm to the list of polygons behind P.

Time Complexity

You need to answer this question to get the time complexity.

How to bound the number of recursive calls?

Recursive calls give rise to new recursive calls (splitting), the expected number is bounded by expected number of fragments. The time complexity can be pretty fine to pretty catastrophic, depending on the space being mapped.

The time consumed for building the tree, can be compromised for quicker rendering of the tree.

Traversal

If the current node is a leaf node then:

- render the polygons at the current node.

Else if the viewing location V is in front of the current node then:

1. Render the child BSP tree containing polygons behind the current node

2. Render the polygons at the current node

3. Render the child BSP tree containing polygons in front of the current node

Else if the viewing location V is behind the current node then:

1. Render the child BSP tree containing polygons in front of the current node

2. Render the polygons at the current node

3. Render the child BSP tree containing polygons behind the current node

Else if the viewing location V must be exactly on the plane associated with the current node, then:

1. Render the child BSP tree containing polygons in front of the current node

2. Render the child BSP tree containing polygons behind the current node

Time Complexity

A BSP Tree is traversed in linear time that is O(N) and renders the polygon in a far to near ordering, suitable for the painter's algorithm.

This ensures fast rendering that is the primary motive behind using Binary Space Partitioning trees in real life situations even though generation might be costlier.

C++ Implementation

This is based on the assumption that Object exposes its position, and the Node class is responsible for, and can write on object's position.

In addition, Objects are added in the first node having room to hold it. In case all nodes are full, we create two empty children (if not done yet), each one representing half part of the parent node.

To remove an object from the tree, we have to find it. We will search it in each node recursively, using its position to take the right branch at each step. When found, we just remove it and return.

Retrieving an object from the tree is really fast when it comes to BSP Trees and the best part is, the more the depth of the tree, greater will be the efficiency in terms of data retrieval. All we have to do is to test all object in all the nodes in the interval. If a node is not in the interval, we can dismiss the entire branch in our search

337

Following is the sample implementation in C++ to give you the complete idea:

```cpp
class Object
{
  int pos;
public:
  int position() const;
  int & position();
};

class Node
{
  static const unsigned int depth_max = 32;
  static const unsigned int max_objects = 32;

  const unsigned int depth;
  const int min, max, center;  // geometry of node
  // actual container for object reference
  std::list<Object*> objects;
  // only constructed if actual container is full
  Node *children[2];

  //Constructor to create a child
  Node(Node const &, bool);
  // check if the children are empty as well
  bool isEmpty() const;
public:
  //Constructor to create the first node
  Node(int min, int max);
  ~Node();                        //Destructor

  void addObject(int position, Object *);
  void delObject(Object *);
  void movObject(int newPos, Object *);

  // Get all object in requisite range
  void getObject(int posMin, int posMax, std::list<Object*> &);
};

// Public constructor, to create root node
Node::Node(int min, int max)
```

```
  : depth(0), min(min), max(max), center((min + max) / 2),
  objects(), children(nullptr)
  {}

  Node::~Node()
  {
    delete[] children;
  }

  // Private constructor for constructing children.
  // Compute it own center and range according to the
  // side indicator.
  // side specifies wich parent's side the child will represent.
  Node::Node(Node const & father, bool side)
   : depth(father.depth + 1),
    min(side ? father.min : father.center),
    max(side ? father.center : father.max),
    center((min + max) / 2),
    objects(),
    children(nullptr)
  {}
  bool Node::isEmpty() const
  {
    return !((!objects.empty()) || children ||
            (children[0]->isEmpty() && children[1]->isEmpty()));
  }

  void Node::addObject()
  {
    if (objects.size() > max_objects && depth < max_depth)
    { // if max object is reached but not depth max
      if (!children) children = new Node(...); // create children
      return; // pass to the corresponding child  and return
    }
    // if depth max is reached and even if node is
    // "full", execution continue
    objects.push_back(obj);
    // overthrow the max_objects limit if max depth is reached
  }

  void Node::delObject(Object * obj)
  {

    if (children && children[0]->isEmpty() && children[1]-
  >isEmpty())
```

```cpp
      delete[] children;
      // after a deletion, if both children are empty, delete them.
}
void Node::addObject(int position, Object * obj)
{
  if (objects.size() > max_objects) // if node is full
    if (depth < depth_max) // if we can go deeper
    {
      if (children == nullptr) // if we need to create child
      // we create each child corresponding to their place
        children = new { Node(*this, false), Node(*this, true) };
      // we pass the object to a child, depending on
      // the object's position
      children[ position <= center ? 0 : 1]->addObject(position,
obj);
      return;
    }
  objects.push_back(obj);
  // we add in this node, in the first and last intention
  obj->position() = position;
}

void Node::delObject(Object * obj)
{
  auto found = std::find(objects.begin(), objects.end(), obj);
  // find object
  if (found != objects.end()) // object found
  {
    objects.remove(found); // removed
    return;
  }
  if (children) // check children
  {
    // recursion for corresponding children
    children[obj->position() <= center ? 0 : 1]->delObject(obj);
    if (children[0]->isEmpty() && children[1]->isEmpty())
      delete[] children;
      // if both children are empty, delete them
  }
}

void Node::movObject(int newPos, Object *obj)
{
  auto found = std::find(objects.begin(), objects.end(), obj);
  //find object
```

```cpp
  if (found == objects.end() && children)
  //object not found, go deeper
  {
    // same partition for old and new pos,
    // recursion on the corresponding child
    if (newPos <= center && obj->position() <= center)
      children[0]->movObject(newPos, obj);
    else if (newPos > center && obj->position() > center)
      children[1]->movObject(newPos, obj);

    // remove from the old partition and add to the new one
    else if (newPos <= center && obj->position() > center)
    {
      children[1]->delObject(obj);
      children[0]->addObject(newPos, obj);
    }
    else if (newPos > center && obj->position() <= center)
    {
      children[0]->delObject(obj);
      children[1]->addObject(newPos, obj);
    }
  }
  // object is now in the right place, so update it position
  obj->position() = newPos;
}

void Node::getObject(int posMin, int posMax, std::list<Object *> &
list)
{
  // get all wanted objects in this node
  for (auto it = objects.begin(); it != objects.end(); it++)
    if (it->position() >= posMin && it->position() <= posMax)
      list.push_back(*it);

  if (childrens) // if you can, go deeper
  {
    if (posMin <= center)
      children[0]->getObject(posMin, posMax, list);
    if (posMax > center)
      children[1]->getObject(posMin, posMax, list);
  }
}
```

What makes this worthwhile?

Even though adding, removing, moving might be a little costlier, you may observe substantial gain at every search. As by logic, you may exclude entire branches during search which highly accelerates the process.

Searching efficiently in order to render necessary objects as quick as possible is the primary goal, in its applications.

Binary space partitioning arose from the need of computer graphics to rapidly draw three-dimensional scenes composed of polygons. A simple way to draw such scenes is the painter's algorithm.

This approach has two *disadvantages*:

1. The time required to sort polygons in back to front order.

2. The possibility of errors in overlapping polygons was also high.

To compensate for these disadvantages, the concept of binary space partitioning tree was proposed.

Applications

Since its inception, Binary Space Partition Trees have been found to be of immense use in the following:

- Computer Graphics
- Back face Culling
- Collision detection
- Ray Tracing
- Game engines using BSP trees include the Doom (id Tech 1), Quake (id Tech 2 variant), GoldSrc and Source engines.

Do not forget it brought you the game that revolutionized video games!

By now you must have understood the significance, utility, concept, and application of Binary Space Partition Trees.

342

Insight:

Based on our insights, you may be driven to the thought that Binary Tree are used to represent a 2-dimensional space. The main idea of a Binary Tree is to represent an N-dimensional space by considering an attribute (or a set) that results in 2 options at each step.

Binary Heap

Heap is a binary tree with two special properties:

- It must have all its nodes in specific order
- The shape must be complete.

Keep in mind: We can have duplicate values in a heap - there is no restriction against that.

A heap does not follow the rules of a binary search tree; unlike binary search trees, the left node does not have to be smaller than the right node! The ordering of the child nodes is not important for a heap; the only ordering that matters is the heap-order property, or the ordering of parent nodes compared to their children.

Heap can be broadly classified in two types:

1. Min heap

2. Max heap

Min Heap

A min heap is a heap where every single parent node, including the root, is less than or equal to the value of its children nodes.

The most important property of a min heap is that the node with the smallest, or minimum value, will always be the root node.

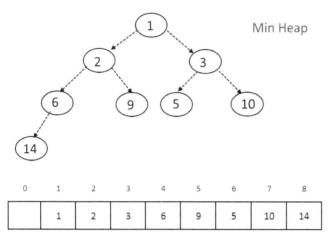

Min Heap

0	1	2	3	4	5	6	7	8
	1	2	3	6	9	5	10	14

for Node at i : Left child will be 2i and right child will be at 2i+1 and parent node will be at [i/2].

Max Heap

A max heap is effectively the converse of a min heap; in this format, every parent node, including the root, is greater than or equal to the value of its children nodes.

The important property of a max heap is that the node with the largest, or maximum value will always be at the root node.

345

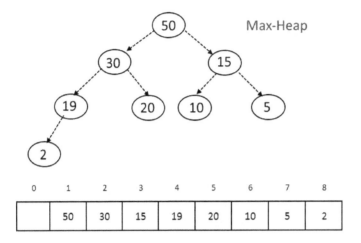

for Node at i : Left child will be 2i and right child will be at 2i+1 and parent node will be at [i/2].

Implementation

- Use array to store the data.
- Start storing from index 1, not 0.
- For any given node at position i:
- Its Left Child is at [2*i] if available.
- Its right child is at [2*i+1] if available.
- Its Parent Node is at [i/2] if available.

This is the implementation of the basic structure of a Binary Heap:

```
public class minHeap {
    public int capacity;
    public int [] mH;
    public int currentSize;
    public minHeap(int capacity){
        this.capacity=capacity;
        mH = new int [capacity+1];
        currentSize =0;
    }
```

346

```
        }
```

Heap has the following fundamental operations:

- Insert Operation(Time complexity O(log N))
- Delete Operation (Time complexity O(log N))
- Extract-Min (OR Extract-Max) (Time complexity O(log N))
- Find-Min (Time complexity O(1))
- Bubble Up/ Bubble down (Sink Down): O(logN)

Bubble-up Operation

Steps:

- If inserted element is smaller than its parent node in case of Min-Heap OR greater than its parent node in case of Max-Heap, swap the element with its parent.
- Keep repeating the above step, if node reaches its correct position, STOP.

Following is the implementation of Bubble Up operation:

```
public void bubbleUp(int pos)
{
        int parentIdx = pos/2;
        int currentIdx = pos;
        while (currentIdx > 0 && mH[parentIdx] > mH[currentIdx])
        {
            swap(currentIdx,parentIdx);
            currentIdx = parentIdx;
            parentIdx = parentIdx/2;
        }
}
```

Insert Operation

Steps:

- Add the element at the bottom leaf of the Heap.

347

- Perform the Bubble-Up operation.
- All Insert Operations must perform the bubble-up operation(it is also called as up-heap, percolate-up, sift-up, trickle-up, heapify-up, or cascade-up)

Pseudocode

```
MIN-HEAP-INSERT(A,key)
heap-size[A] <- heap-size[A] + 1
A[heap-size[A]] <- +inf
HEAP-DECREASE-KEY(A,heap-size[A],key)
```

Following is the implementation of insert operation in Java:

```java
public void insert(int x)
{
        if(currentSize==capacity)
        {
            System.out.println("heap is full");
            return;
        }
        currentSize++;
        int idx = currentSize;
        mH[idx] = x;
        bubbleUp(idx);
}
```

Sink-Down Operation

Steps:

- If replaced element is greater than any of its child node in case of Min-Heap OR smaller than any if its child node in case of Max-Heap, swap the element with its smallest child(Min-Heap) or with its greatest child(Max-Heap).
- Keep repeating the above step, if node reaches its correct position, STOP.

Pseudocode:

348

```
HEAP-DECREASE-KEY(A,i,key)

if key > A[i]

then error ''new key is larger than current key''

A[i] <- key

while i > 1 and A[parent(i)] > A[i]

do exchange A[i] <-> A[parent(i)]

i <- parent(i)
```

Following is the implementation of Sink Down operation in Java:

```java
public void sinkDown(int k)
{
        int smallest = k;
        int leftChildIdx = 2 * k;
        int rightChildIdx = 2 * k+1;
        if (leftChildIdx < heapSize() &&
            mH[smallest] > mH[leftChildIdx]) {
            smallest = leftChildIdx;
        }
        if (rightChildIdx < heapSize() &&
            [smallest] > mH[rightChildIdx]) {
            smallest = rightChildIdx;
        }
        if (smallest != k) {
            swap(k, smallest);
            sinkDown(smallest);
        }
}
```

Extract-Min OR Extract-Max Operation

Steps:

• Take out the element from the root.(it will be minimum in case of Min-Heap and maximum in case of Max-Heap).

- Take out the last element from the last level from the heap and replace the root with the element.
- Perform Sink-Down.

All delete operation must perform Sink-Down Operation (also known as bubble-down, percolate-down, sift-down, trickle down, heapify-down, cascade-down).

Pseudocode:

```
HEAP-EXTRACT-MIN(A)
if heap-size[A] < 1
then error ''heap underflow''
min <- A[1]
A[1] <- A[heap-size[A]]
heap-size[A] <- heap-size[A] - 1
MIN-HEAPIFY(A,1)
return min
```

Following is the implementation of extract min operation in Java:

```
public int extractMin()
{
        int min = mH[1];
        mH[1] = mH[currentSize];
        mH[currentSize] = 0;
        sinkDown(1);
        currentSize--;
        return min;
}
```

Delete Operation

Steps:

- Find the index for the element to be deleted.

350

- Take out the last element from the last level from the heap and replace the index with this element .
- Perform Sink-Down.

Try to implement Delete operation on your own as you must have the complete idea now.

Applications

The heap data structure has many applications:

- Heapsort: One of the best sorting methods being in-place and with no quadratic worst-case scenarios.
- Selection algorithms: A heap allows access to the min or max element in constant time, and other selections (such as median or kth-element) can be done in sub-linear time on data that is in a heap.
- Graph algorithms: By using heaps as internal traversal data structures, run time will be reduced by polynomial order. Examples of such problems are Prim's minimal-spanning-tree algorithm and Dijkstra's shortest-path algorithm.
- Priority Queue: A priority queue is an abstract concept like "a list" or "a map"; just as a list can be implemented with a linked list or an array, a priority queue can be implemented with a heap or a variety of other methods.
- K-way merge: A heap data structure is useful to merge many already-sorted input streams into a single sorted output stream. Examples of the need for merging include external sorting and streaming results from distributed data such as a log structured merge tree. The inner loop is obtaining the min element, replacing with the next element for the corresponding input stream, then doing a sift-down heap operation. (Alternatively, the replace function.) (Using extract-max and insert functions of a priority queue are much less efficient.)
- Order statistics: The Heap data structure can be used to efficiently find the kth smallest (or largest) element in an array.

Insight:

Binary Heap is important when compared to other variants of Binary Tree because this illustrates how we can represent a Binary Tree using an array.

351

Hence, array and linked list are two fundamental data structures and Binary Tree builds over it by removing the linear nature and bringing in the branching nature.

Treap

A Treap is a height balanced binary tree.

It is used to store a sequence in a tree, which allows for various applications like searching. A Cartesian tree (a Binary Search Tree variant) in case of a sorted sequence, would be basically a linked list, making tree virtually useless. (*Think of this with BST*)

Treap is used to solve such cases by using random priority for each node.

Thus, treap is a balanced binary tree with heap properties.

A treap node stores 2 values:

- Key (Sequence element)
- Priority

A treap is built in such a way that it is essentially a binary search tree for Keys, that is the sequence elements and a heap for priorities. So, a treap follows following properties:

- Priority of a node is always greater than its children.
- The key of a node is greater than the key stored in its left child.
- The key of a node is lower than the key stored in its right child.

The priority for each sequence element is chosen randomly. The insertion process is essentially to create a node as leaf with random priority and perform tree rotations to repair any violations of heap property.

Following is the node structure of Treap:

```
struct Node
{
    int key, priority;
    Node *left, *right;
    Node(int x)
    {
        key = x;
```

```
        priority = rand() % 10000;
        left = right = NULL;
    }
};
```

Tree rotation operation:

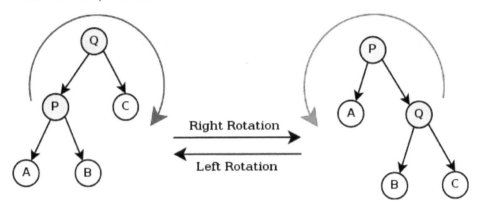

In the above image, A, B, C are subtrees, while P and Q are two nodes that are target of rotation. The left image shows right rotation of node P while image on right shows right rotation of node Q. These two operations are inverse of each other.

Following are the implementations of the left rotate and right rotate operations:

```
Node * rotateLeft(Node *p)
{
    Node *q = p->right;

    p->right = q->left;
    q->left = p;

    return q;
}

Node * rotateRight(Node *q)
{
    Node *p = q->left;

    q->left = p->right;
    p->right = q;
```

354

```
        return p;
}
```

A treap is expected to perform three major operations:

- Search
- Insert
- Delete

Inorder traversal of a treap would give the sorted sequence.

Algorithm

Insert operation

Insert operation is done for the whole sequence to build the tree.

1. Create new node with the given key value x and random priority value.

2. Start from root and perform search for x by using key values to perform a binary search. When a leaf node is reached, insert new node at the leaf. This is basically a binary search tree insertion.

3. Rotate up to make sure heap property is satisfied with respect to priority values.

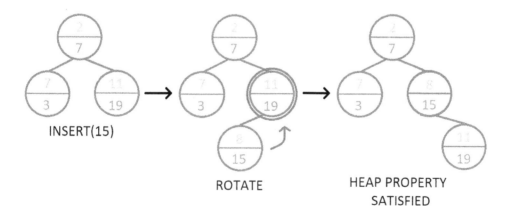

INSERT(15)

ROTATE

HEAP PROPERTY
SATISFIED

The image above shows insert operation for key 15. Green values in nodes are keys and orange values are priorities. Priority of 8 is assigned to node with key 15 randomly.

Following is the implementation of Insert operation:

```
Node * insert(Node *sub_tree, int key)
{
        // If leaf is reached
        if(sub_tree == NULL)
            return new Node(key);

        if(sub_tree->key < key)
        {
            // Run insert for right sub-tree
            sub_tree->right = insert(sub_tree->right, key);

            // Check if right subtree satisfies min-heap property
            if(sub_tree->right->priority < sub_tree->priority)
            {
                // Perform left rotate
                sub_tree = rotateLeft(sub_tree);

            }
        }
        else
        {
            // Run insert for left sub-tree
            sub_tree->left = insert(sub_tree->left, key);

            // Check if left subtree satisfies min-heap property
            if(sub_tree->left->priority < sub_tree->priority)
            {
                // Perform right rotate
                sub_tree = rotateRight(sub_tree);
            }
        }
        return sub_tree;
}
```

Search operation

356

Search operation is same as search in binary search tree since rotation maintains BST property.

1. Start from root to search for a key x.

2. Compare key of the node. If key is equal to x, return the node.

3. If key is less than x go to right child and repeat step 2.

4. If key is greater than x go to left child and repeat step 2.

5. If key is not equal to x and node has no children, then x is not present in tree.

Following is the implementation of search operation in C++:

```
Node * search(Node *sub_tree, int key)
{
        if(sub_tree == NULL)
            return NULL;

        if(sub_tree->key == key)
            return sub_tree;
        else if(sub_tree->key < key)
        {
            return(search(sub_tree->right, key));
        }
        else return(search(sub_tree->left, key));
}
```

Delete operation

1. Search for the node to be deleted.

2. If the node is at leaf, delete it directly.

3. Otherwise, set the node to lowest priority and perform rotations until heap property of tree is satisfied.

4. Delete the node when it is at leaf.

For step 3, if tree is a max heap, set node's priority to negative infinity and

357

if tree is a min heap, set priority to infinity.

The time and space complexity of different operations in Treap are as follows:

- Space complexity: O(N)
- Search: O(logN)
- Insert: O(logN)
- Delete: O(logN)

Applications

- Treap is used as a self-balancing binary tree.
- Treap is used to solve connectivity problems.

Insight:

Treap is an important variant of Binary Tree as it illustrates how randomness can be incorporated in a Data Structure and still manage to make it useful in an efficient way. In fact, several Data Structures that are used in practice are probabilistic in nature.

Can you think of other ways that we can make Binary Tree work randomly in a specific direction?

Some real problems

Problem 1: Represent Excel sheet

Given an excel sheet as a grid of cells, we can store data in a cell. We support two operations:

- Deletion of a particular cell
- Insertion of data in a particular cell

What data structure will you use? How will you implement the operations?

The answer is **Binary Tree**.

This can be tricky at first but once you realize this, you can solve the vast range of problems.

As excel sheet can be of a vast size with empty cells, using an array or linked list will result in significant wastage of space. Additionally, operations will depend on the total size supported by our structure.

Each cell is represented by x and y coordinates (x, y).

The idea is "Each cell will be a node of Binary Tree".

If cell X is on the left side of cell Y, then X will be the left child node of Y or X will be in the left sub-tree of Y.

Inserting a new node will require you to check the correct position in the Binary Tree and will be similar to inserting element in Binary Search Tree. The operation will depend on the total number of elements.

It is advised to use a self-balancing Binary Search Tree.

359

Similarly, for deletion, we need to check if any node is impacted by the deletion. Note that if data is stored in the node, it needs to be deleted from the Binary Tree. Further, we need to check if other nodes are impacted as if a cell is deleted, other cells are shifted by one accordingly.

We need to adjust coordinates of all such cell accordingly.

The time complexity of the operations will be:

- Insertion: O(logN) in worst case;
- Deletion: O(N) in worst case; O(logN) on average.

N is the number of cells with data.

In a real excel sheet, we will be using a more complex data structure but using Binary Tree is the first step. All improvements come from this stage.

Problem 2: Find Available Memory

When we allocate memory to a data structure, the system needs to find an available space in the memory, and this takes time. If a memory address is of N bits, then there will be 2^N memory addresses or 2^N bytes of memory.

Memory is often fragmented that is memory is allocated sequentially but as parts of memory is deleted, there are empty space in between allocated memory and this part cannot be allocated if the requested space is more.

Hence, if you were to design this memory system, how will you design the memory allocation system.

We can use a Self-balancing Binary Search Tree.

Each node is a continuous memory chunk and is denoted by the amount of memory available in the chunk and has the starting and ending address as its attribute. For every chunk, we create a node and insert it into the tree.

Note: Initially, when no memory is allocated, then there will be only one node.

When a memory is requested, we will traverse our tree to find the node which has the smallest memory available such that it satisfies the requested memory.

On allocation, we will update the node and its attributes if some memory of the chunk is left. After updating, we need to move it to its correct position which should not take more than O(logM) time where M is the number of chunks.

If no memory is left, the node is deleted, and its child nodes are adjusted accordingly.

Hence, if we design our memory allocator using a Binary Tree, we will achieve the following time and space complexity:

* Memory allocation: **O(logM)**

where M is the number of chunks. M cannot be greater than 2N that is the total available memory and hence, logM will be N at most where N is the number of bits in the address.

As N is constant for a system (64 for a 64-bit system), we can assume that our approach is taking nearly constant time.

Problem 3: Cache

Cache is a copy of certain elements that can be accessed quickly as memory access of main memory is time consuming. Cache needs to maintain the copy such that access is quick.

One idea is that frequently accessed elements is more likely to be accessed again and hence, should be close.

Designing a cache is a common problem and using a Binary Tree is one solution.

The approach should be to use Splay Tree which is a Self-balancing Binary Tree with the property that recently accessed elements are closer to the root.

361

Though, the time complexity will be same as an usual Binary Tree but in practice, Splay Tree will perform much better.

If you need to find an element at index T, then we can merge the properties of Binary Search Tree with Splay Tree to improve performance better.

You have the knowledge of both Binary Search Tree and Splay Tree, so you should think at this point:

How will you modify the operations of Splay Tree to make it act as a Binary Search Tree?

Another approach is to use: **Binary Heap**.

We have explored Max and Min Heap. Similarly, instead of giving priority to the relative value of a node, we need to consider the number of times the value has been accessed.

This will make the most accessed element to be accessed in constant time $O(1)$.

This may not be the best solution in general but for specific caches, this approach may work better than other alternatives.

For this problem of designing a cache, there are other viable options like Linked Lists, Priority Queue, Priority Heap and much more.

You shall consider all types and then, choose a specific approach for your problem at hand.

Applications & Concluding Note

If you have reached this point, you have a strong hold on Binary Tree concepts and are ready to dive deeper into Advanced Topics and conduct your own Independent Research in Data Structures.

Some of the applications of Binary Tree and variants are:

- Binary Tree is used to as the basic data structure in Microsoft Excel and spreadsheets in usual.
- Binary Tree is used to implement indexing of Segmented Database.
- Splay Tree (Binary Tree variant) is used in implemented efficient cache is hardware and software systems.
- Binary Space Partition Trees are used in Computer Graphics, Back face Culling, Collision detection, Ray Tracing and algorithms in rendering game graphics.
- Syntax Tree (Binary Tree with nodes as operations) are used to compute arithmetic expressions in compilers like GCC, AOCL and others.
- Binary Heap (Binary Tree variant of Heap) is used to implement Priority Queue efficiently which in turn is used in Heap Sort Algorithm.
- Binary Search Tree is used to search elements efficiently and used as a collision handling technique in Hash Map implementations.
- Balanced Binary Search Tree is used to represent memory to enable fast memory allocation.
- Huffman Tree (Binary Tree variant) is used internally in a Greedy Algorithm for Data Compression known as Huffman Encoding and Decoding.
- Merkle Tree/ Hash Tree (Binary Tree variant) is used in Blockchain implementations and p2p programs requiring signatures.
- Binary Tries (Tries with 2 child) is used to represent a routing data which vacillate efficient traversal.
- Morse code is used to encode data and uses a Binary Tree in its representation.
- Goldreich, Goldwasser and Micali (GGM) Tree (Binary Tree variant) is used compute pseudorandom functions using an arbitrary pseudorandom generator.
- Scapegoat tree (a self-balancing Binary Search Tree) is used in implementing Paul-Carole games to model a faulty search process.

363

- Treap (radomized Binary Search Tree) is used to solve connectivity problems in Network systems.

As you must have noted, there are several other variants of Binary Tree (as listed in the applications) which we have not covered as they are advanced topics, but we have presented the core ideas in the problems we have covered.

Hence, if you just read the basic idea of a particular variant, you can easily figure out the details of different operations. Try this will *"Scapegoat Tree"*.

The general idea is: We will not keep doing small operations to keep the Binary Tree self-balanced as with AA Tree and Splay Tree.

instead, if we notice that something goes wrong, then we will find the node who is responsible for it ("scapegoat") and completely, rebuild the sub-tree.

Work on this idea independently.

Why is Binary Tree is so widely used?

Binary Tree is the most widely used Data Structure because:

- Binary Tree is the simplest and most efficient data structure to be used in most Software Systems. It is the properties of Binary Tree that makes it so widely used.
- N-ary Tree which is the generalization of Binary Tree is complex to implement and is rarely a better fit.
- Binary Tree can be implemented as an array using ideas of Binary Heap. Hence, the ideas of OOP (Object Oriented Programming) are not necessary for a safe implementation.
- There is a wide range of variants of Binary Tree which makes it very likely to find a suitable variant for a specific problem. For example, if we want a Data Structure where recently accessed elements are closer to the beginning of the data structure so that access is fast, then we have a variant of Binary Tree known as Splay Tree.

Alternatives to Binary Tree

364

Despite the wide use of Binary Tree, there are a few Data Structures that have found strong use case and Binary Tree cannot replace them in terms of performance.

Alternatives to Binary Trees include:

- B-Tree and B+ Tree: used in indexing of database
- Space Partitioning Tree: For higher dimensional games
- Quadtree
- Tree pyramid (T-pyramid)
- Octree
- k-d (K dimensional) tree
- R-tree: to find shortest path or nearby objects in 3D graphs

With this, you have a strong idea of Binary Tree. You can confidently ace every Problem related to Binary Tree at Coding Interviews of Top Companies and swim through Hard Competitive Coding Problems.

As a next step, you may randomly pick a problem from this book, read the problem statement and dive into designing your own solution and implement it in a Programming Language of your choice.

You may need to revise the concepts present in this book again in two months to strengthen your practice.

Remember, we are here to help you. If you have any doubts in a problem, you can contact us by email (team@opengenus.org) anytime.

Best of Luck.

If you want more practice, feel free to join our Internship Program:

internship.OPENGENUS.org

Aditya Chatterjee

Srishti Guleria

Ue Kiao

iq.OPENGENUS.org

www.ingramcontent.com/pod-product-compliance
Lightning Source LLC
Chambersburg PA
CBHW080613060326
40690CB00021B/4677